Mindfulness

Be mindful. Live in the moment.

Gill Hasson

CAPSTONE
A Wiley Brand

For my Dad who died while I was writing this book.
He always knew that the present moment is life itself.

Contents

Introduction   1

How Mindful Are You?   11

Part One: Understanding Mindfulness   **17**

1 Why be Mindful?   19

2 Moving Towards Mindful Thinking   33

3 Mindful Thinking and Feeling   59

4 Mindful Doing   75

Part Two: Putting It into Practice   **95**

5 Managing Painful Emotions: Anger,
Worry and Anxiety, Guilt   99

6 Mindfulness for Self-Esteem: Confidence,
Self-Esteem and Loneliness   125

7 Mindful Motivation: Goals and Willpower   141

8 Mindfulness with Others: Listening,
Managing Criticism, Forgiving, Persuading and
Motivating   159

9 Mindfulness at Work: Interviews,
Meetings and Presentations   181

Conclusion   195

References   197

About the Author   199

Acknowledgements   201

Index   203

Introduction

Recently, I listened to a palliative care nurse talking about her work with terminally ill patients. She explained that a key aspect of her work was to help provide a sense of "now" for the dying; to enable people to make the most of their time; to live their life with purpose, dignity and support; to make the most of the present, rather than getting too caught up in regrets for the past or fears for the future.

Her work is clearly meaningful and valuable. But listening to this nurse, it made me wonder why so many people might wait till they're dying to learn how to make "now" such an important part of their life.

From the moment we're born, now is *always* what we have. There is never a time when our lives are not now, in this moment. The present moment is, in fact, life itself!

Life unfolds in the present.

As George Harrison once said: "It's being here now that's important. There's no past and there's no future . . . all there is ever, is the now. We can gain experience from the past, but we can't relive it; and we can hope for the future, but we don't know if there is one."

How can *you* make the most of "now"? By learning to be mindful.

You may think that being mindful requires an ability to completely clear your mind and go off into an altered state in an attempt to get to a better place. Not so; mindfulness does not involve complex meditation routines. Mindfulness is *not* about having an empty mind or suppressing thoughts and feelings. Nor does it require years of practice, sitting in the lotus position in a flowing white robe on a beautiful beach.

There are two ways of practising mindfulness; the formal way and the informal way.

Formal mindfulness is probably better known as meditation; it involves following established practices; taking time out of your day to be still and silent, to focus on your breath, to be aware of sounds, senses, thoughts and feelings.

Informal mindfulness requires no conventions. It simply means bringing mindful awareness to everyday life; to daily activities such as eating, walking, driving and housework. Informal mindfulness is also part of your interactions with other people; at work, at home and in your social life.

This book is concerned with *informal* mindfulness – it is about mindfulness outside of meditation.

Your mind is able to think back and reflect on past events and experiences. Your mind can also think about the future; it can plan ahead.

Of course, your mind can wander to good things; you can remember good times and anticipate forthcoming events. But this ability to think back to the past and forward to the future is not always an unmitigated blessing.

Too often, life is racing by. There's no time to experience what's happening now, because you're busy thinking about what needs doing tomorrow or you're distracted by thoughts about what did or didn't happen yesterday. And all the time your mind is chattering with commentary or judgement.

Other times you can get stuck in the past, going back over and over events or becoming paralyzed by worries about the future.

Why mindfulness is so relevant to our lives now

At its most extreme, worrying about the future can lead to anxiety disorders. Dwelling on the past can lead to depression.

Research[1] shows that the number of people in England who experience depression and anxiety has slowly but steadily risen in the last 20 years.

In 1993, depression with anxiety was experienced by 7.5% of the population, rising to 9.7% in 2007. Generalized anxiety disorder was experienced by 4.45% of the population in 1993 rising to 4.7% in 2007.

Feeling overwhelmed by the past or the future takes us away from living in the now, in the present. Too often, we let the present slip away. It's easy to waste "now" time, missing what is happening in the only moment that really exists.

When you're at work, for example, you're thinking about being on holiday; on holiday, you're worrying about the work piling up on your desk.

Nowadays, to make matters worse, you can take your phone and computer on holiday with you so that wherever you go, you are never actually there! Computers, smart phones, MP3 players; there are plenty of ways that modern technology can make you lose touch with what is happening and where you are right now.

Mindfulness enables you to experience and appreciate your life instead of rushing through it, constantly trying to be somewhere else.

> "Mindfulness is the ultimate mobile device; you can use it anywhere, anytime, unobtrusively."
> Sharon Salzberg

Mindfulness is a way of living your life so that you are in the present moment more often. It involves bringing your awareness back from the future or the past and into the present moment. You are not trying to get to a better place or to become a better person – you are already there.

Mindfulness is living *in* the moment, not living *for* the moment.

When you are living *for* the moment, there are no potential consequences. You do something that makes you feel good right now, in this moment. But often, it's a surprise to find out that there are consequences to pay!

When you are living *in* the moment, you know that this moment leads to the next one; that life is a series of connected moments. You make conscious decisions – based on your beliefs and values – and you take responsibility for your choices.

About this book

This book is in two parts: Part One helps you to understand mindfulness; what it involves and how you can learn to be more mindful.

We start by asking "How Mindful Are You?" to get you thinking about where your mind is at in a variety of situations.

In Chapter 1 you will discover the benefits of mindfulness – how mindfulness can have a positive effect in different areas of your life. Chapter 2 will help you to understand how and why you might slip into being mind*less* instead of mind*ful*. You will learn ways to change how you think and you'll discover that simply being aware of how you use your mind is being mindful.

You'll be encouraged to open yourself to new ideas and ways of doing things; to let go of unhelpful ways of thinking and establish more helpful, mindful ways of thinking.

You will find out that you *can* change the way you think.

But whatever it is that you think, your thoughts come with emotions and feelings attached to them. In fact, thoughts and feelings are inextricably linked. Chapter 3 focuses on being more aware of your emotions in order to break free from unhelpful thoughts and thinking patterns.

So far, we have focused on thoughts and feelings.

So in Chapter 4 we turn to being mindful of what you *do*. You will see that mindfulness is most easily practised by turning everyday activities into opportunities for mindfulness. There are plenty of ideas, tips and techniques to help you apply mindfulness to the everyday activities of your life.

You'll be encouraged to bring your attention to a new level by slowing down whatever you're doing. You will see that you only have to spend a few minutes each day doing mindfully those activities that you usually hurry through. Everyday activities like washing up or brushing your teeth.

Each of these everyday activities gives you an opportunity to be mindful. These opportunities raise your awareness. Then, from practising these little awarenesses, you can develop a more whole experience of mindfulness itself.

It's all very optimistic and encouraging and that theme continues as we end Part 1 on a high note; you are urged to actively seek out the good things in life.

How is that mindful?

Because making an effort to notice the good things in life – the small pleasures and the people and things that make a positive difference to you – is, in itself, being mindful. You bring your awareness to how good you feel right now, in the present moment. Noticing what is good right now *is* living in the moment.

Having developed a clear understanding of what mindfulness is and how to be mindful, in Part 2, we turn to specific situations where being mindful can really help you.

You will learn how being mindful can help you to be less swept away by thoughts and behaviour that lead to stress, self-doubt, depression and anxiety. You will see how to apply mindfulness in your relationships with other people and you will learn how mindfulness techniques can help with your own personal development.

You'll notice that the same principles arise throughout – acknowledge and accept, focus and engage, let go and begin again etc. Each time you apply these principles, each time you approach a situation with mindfulness, you are learning how to relate more directly to your life.

"Yesterday is gone. Tomorrow has not yet come. We have only today. Let us begin."
Mother Teresa

How Mindful Are You?

How often do you live mindfully, meeting each moment of life as it presents itself, with full awareness, without judging it? If you're like most people, often you are trying to do two or three things at once. And you probably do most things automatically, without noticing what you're doing.

Perhaps, for example, you've decided to make yourself some tea; as you wait for the kettle to boil you either start doing something else – reading the paper, washing up, making a phone call – or maybe you start thinking about a conversation you had yesterday or look in the fridge planning what to have for dinner tonight. Your mind is not on the tea – it's not on what's happening right now.

It's easy to get so caught up in your thoughts and feelings about the past or future that, without realizing it, you've disconnected from what is happening right now in front of you.

Ok, so missing the full tea experience is not that big a deal! There are, of course, times when being able to think of more than two things at once allows you to get a lot done quickly and efficiently.

The real difficulties arise, however, when your mind gets lost in stressful thoughts about the past and the future: replaying painful experiences from the past and imagining worst-case scenarios about the future. At its most extreme, being stuck in the past leads to depression and being trapped in the future leads to anxiety.

Or, it may be that what's happening right now is painful. In those circumstances, you may live in denial; avoiding painful feelings and situations that you can't accept or bear to live with.

All this rewinding back to the past and fast forwarding to the future is exhausting and rarely productive.

Which of these situations are familiar to you?

1. Often, I experience an emotion – guilt, jealousy, resentment – but I'm not aware until sometime later.
2. When I'm doing routine things such as supermarket shopping, waiting for a bus, washing up or making dinner I'm usually thinking of something else.
3. I often find it difficult to motivate myself or summon up enough willpower to do what I told myself I would.
4. I tend to walk quickly to get where I'm going and don't notice my surroundings as I pass by.
5. I'm not usually aware of how physically tense I am at times.
6. I often feel that I'm just spinning from one situation to another. "Stop the world I want to get off" is a feeling I have.
7. I'm often thinking about what else needs doing next week or what I failed to do yesterday.

8. My mind is usually chattering with commentary or judgement about events or other people.
9. I do jobs or tasks automatically, without being aware of what I'm doing.
10. I sometimes find myself listening to someone with one ear and doing something else at the same time.
11. I drive places on "automatic pilot" and just focus on getting there.
12. I sometimes wish time away – impatient for a future event to occur.
13. I sometimes find myself going back over past hurts. I find it difficult to forgive.
14. I often interrupt or am thinking about something else when someone is talking to me.
15. Quite often, I feel bogged down with routine.
16. My work is either boring or stressful.
17. I rarely find a hobby, sport or pastime that absorbs me and that I enjoy fully.
18. I sometimes feel detached and disconnected from other people. It makes me unhappy.
19. I often feel guilty. If I screw up I give myself a hard time. I keep going back over what I should or shouldn't have done.
20. I lack confidence and self-esteem.

The more often you answer yes, the more areas of your life can benefit from mindfulness. Read on!

PART ONE

Understanding Mindfulness

1
Why be Mindful?

There's nothing mystical about mindfulness. To be mindful simply means to be aware and engage with what's happening right now. It's about being in the moment.

If you've ever become absorbed in a crossword puzzle or a board game, sung your heart out or "lost" yourself in a book or a film, a letter you were writing or work that you were doing – then you've experienced mindfulness; you've been totally in the moment.

Children are great role models for being in the moment. Watch a child as he plays; he's not thinking about what happened yesterday, or what he's going to do later today. He's simply absorbed in what he's drawing, making or pretending to be. When he's upset, he yells and cries – nothing else matters but what has upset him. He'll cry about it, and then let it go; the offending situation gone and forgotten.

Have you ever taken small children to the cinema? Everything is new and amazing. They stare at the bright lights in the foyer. They stare at everyone sitting around them. They move the seats up and down, gawp at the big screen and flinch when the music starts. They jump on to your lap when it gets scary and they laugh out loud when it's funny. They live each moment.

Even cats show us how to live in the moment! When I look at our cat Norman, I'm sure he's not thinking about the new brand of cat food he had for breakfast or worrying about what's for dinner. Norman simply lives from moment to moment.

You can become mindful at any moment. You can do it right now. Stop everything. Focus on what's happening. What can you hear? What can you smell? Look straight ahead; what do you see? What can you feel? What can you taste?

Don't give it any thought; you don't need to like or dislike, approve or disapprove of what's happening. You simply need to be aware of it.

Even if nothing is there, just be aware of your breathing; the sensation of the air as it enters your nose or mouth and fills your lungs, and as it goes out again.

Does all this seem a bit pointless? How can this non-doing approach be of any value? Let me explain.

The ability to think; to think back on past events and to think about the future – to plan ahead – is a feature that defines us as humans. As well as being capable of thinking about things that *are* happening, we can think about:

- things that *did and didn't* happen
- things that *have* happened
- things that *might* happen
- things that may *never* happen at all.

But thinking is not always an unmitigated blessing. Too often, your thoughts can trap you; trap you in the past and trap you in the future.

If you're ruminating about events and going back over them again and again then you're living in the past. You're trapped there. Other times, you can be fretting about what lies ahead; anxious and worried: you're trapped in the future. And all the time your mind is chattering with commentary or judgement.

What occurs as a result is that there's no time to experience what's happening right now, because you're distracted by what may happen tomorrow and next week or maybe you're too busy worrying about what you did or failed to do yesterday.

Even when nothing much is happening, *something* is happening. Typically for most of us, it is thinking. Thinking is happening. Rather than simply being aware of what's happening, we're thinking about what is – or is not – happening.

Thinking seems to be our default setting.

If you've ever tried to meditate, the first thing you will notice is that your mind has a life of its own. It just goes on and on: thinking, musing, fantasizing, planning, anticipating, worrying, liking, disliking, remembering, forgetting, evaluating, reacting and so on.

A recent study[2] found that people spend half their waking hours thinking about something other than what they're actually doing, and this mind-wandering typically makes them unhappy.

The research, by psychologists Matthew A. Killingsworth and Daniel T. Gilbert of Harvard University, used an iPhone Web app to gather 250,000 data points on peoples' thoughts, feelings and actions as they went about their lives.

"A human mind is a wandering mind, and a wandering mind is an unhappy mind" Killingsworth and Gilbert write. "The ability to think about what is *not* happening is a cognitive achievement that comes at an emotional cost."

They discovered that our minds are wandering about 46.9% of the time in any given activity, and the mind-wandering rate was at least 30% for all but one activity. The only activity that generally got people's undivided attention was having sex. (Really? Not sure that I believe that bit!)

The study discovered that people's feelings of happiness had much more to do with where their mind was than what they were doing.

People consistently reported being happiest when their minds were actually on what they were doing.

In his book, *The Power of Now*, Eckhart Tolle suggests that your mind is a superb instrument if used correctly. Used incorrectly, however, it becomes destructive. "It is not so much that you use your mind wrongly – you usually don't use it at all. It uses you. This is the disease. You believe that you are your mind. This is the delusion. The instrument has taken you over."

Certainly, your mind can wander to good things. You can remember good times and anticipate upcoming events. Mind-wandering becomes a problem though when you are ruing the past, or worrying about the future.

But, the past is gone and the future isn't here yet. What exists between past and future is the present moment.

So how can mindfulness help?

Mindfulness is a way to look after your mind. Your mind thinks all day and dreams at night. It's always busy and you expect it to just keep going. You cannot stop the mind from thinking, but if it's not given rest, it won't function well.

Mindfulness can give you a break from the endless chatter going on in your mind. It's a bit like the commentary that comes with a sports programme on the TV. Two things are happening: firstly, the game itself and secondly the endless commentary. Turn off the sound and you can experience the game in a more direct way rather than through the mind of another. In your own life, your thoughts are doing the commentary, interpreting your experience: how hard it is, how great it is, how unfair, how beautiful, how wrong, how boring and so on.

Too often, you can get swept away by a tidal wave of thoughts and feelings. This can be particularly powerful when you are faced with worries, pressures and responsibilities and wanting things to be different.

Being mindful; paying attention to what is happening in the present moment is a welcome relief from these stressful and habitual thought patterns.

Mindfulness keeps you grounded and centred – less pushed by what's going on around you. You are more able to stay focused and be calmly present in the midst of both pleasant and unpleasant experiences.

It's not easy to "think straight" when your mind is over-whelmed and confused; it's hard to see through the mental clutter. Mindfulness helps you to make clear decisions more easily; to choose between one course of action and another.

However, this does not mean that you become rigid in your thinking and behaviour. Quite the opposite! Mindfulness allows you be more flexible with your thinking. When you're aware of how and what you are thinking, you will be able to disengage from established ways of responding and be open to new, more helpful ways.

You will find that when you are mindful you are less critical. Mindfulness frees you from judgement; it allows you to experience something without judging, assessing or analyzing. You are able to observe experience without getting caught up in it. You understand that what's happening is only difficult, bad, wrong etc. if you choose to think of it as such.

In fact, mindfulness helps you to be aware of when your thinking and self-talk have slipped into negative and unhelpful patterns; to know the type of thoughts and self-talk that fuel your emotions.

When you are mindful, you are more attuned to the links between your thoughts, feelings and behaviour. You are less reactive and more responsive. What's the difference? Well, if you *react*, you are likely to resist or oppose what is happening. If you *respond*, you behave in a way that is appropriate to the situation.

For example, if you feel you have behaved badly towards someone, you might react by attempting to justify your behaviour or deny that you did anything wrong. When you are mindful, you are aware of how you feel and what those feelings are telling you. As a result, you are more likely to respond to those feelings of guilt by putting right what you did wrong.

Mindfulness can help you manage a range of difficult emotions. It can help you, for example, to reduce and manage anxiety and worry. When you are focused on the present – on what is happening right now – it is not possible for worries and anxieties to come charging into your head.

Mindfulness is also a powerful way to prevent anger from getting out of control; you are more aware of the warning signs and able to manage the impulse to react immediately. You discover that everything slows down in a way that helps you to respond to difficult situations in a much calmer way.

The quality of your life improves – you are able to manage difficult situations more easily and get more out of the good things in life.

Mindfulness allows you to become totally absorbed in something and enjoy what you are experiencing. You are so focused on what's happening right now, that there is no thought of the "next" moment; nothing can distract you.

You are able to let go and turn your attention to the things that make life worth living.

Mindfulness frees you from being preoccupied with your own situation. Your mind opens to the world unfolding right before you – the singing of the birds, the changing light, the movement of traffic; whatever it is in front of your eyes that is happening right now. It doesn't matter how many times the birds have sung, the light has changed or the traffic has passed by, mindfulness can help you to see things differently; you are open to new possibilities even in familiar situations.

In fact, mindfulness turns a boring or routine activity into something new. It creates a new perspective; a new way of looking at things and gives you the opportunity to experience everything as if it's for the first time. It doesn't matter how often you've done something, it will always be different; there will always be a different way to do something.

And so, because you are open to new experiences, mindfulness allows you to let go of anything that limits possibilities. It gives you confidence and courage. You develop a stronger self-belief; you are positive about your abilities and are more able to fulfil your good intentions and achieve your goals.

There's no room for self-doubt, no room for unhelpful self-talk such as "I'll never be able to do this", or "I'm not good enough". Mindfulness increases your awareness of these judgemental thoughts; how unhelpful they are and how bad they make you feel.

You put aside the judgements and conclusions you came to as a result of past behaviour and instead think about what you learned that could help you do things differently the next time.

Last but by no means least, mindfulness helps you to understand and connect with other people more effectively. How? In so many ways. You are more able to engage with other people because you are focused on them; you are less distracted and more able to listen to what they're saying and feeling. You are more aware of other people's needs and feelings, you are able to experience and understand another person's situation from their perspective. You are more accepting of other people and the differences between you and there is an increased understanding between you. It's a win–win situation!

However, if being mindful simply means to be aware and to engage with what's happening right now, you might wonder how being mindful can be so helpful in such a wide range of situations. It's because there are several aspects and principles of mindfulness.

Aspects of mindfulness

Awareness. This involves being conscious and alert to thoughts, experience and events that are happening in the present moment.

Acknowledgement. This is the recognition of the existence of something. With mindfulness, this means recognizing thoughts, feelings, experiences and events *are* occurring.

Acceptance. This is the state of not doing anything, just understanding that things are (or are not) happening. Acceptance involves knowing that thoughts, feelings, sensations, beliefs and actions, are just that; thoughts, feelings, sensations and beliefs. It's in the present moment that acceptance occurs.

Non-judgemental. This means not making an evaluation of what is happening, just simply experiencing, or observing it. Being non-judgemental requires that you do not give any meaning to your thoughts and feelings, other peoples' actions and events. You simply look at things in an objective way as opposed to seeing them as either "good" or "bad". It's only when you attach thoughts to experiences and events that they have any meaning.

Letting go. This means not hanging on or getting attached to thoughts, feelings, ideas and events. Recognizing they are part of the past.

Focus and engagement. Mindfulness requires focus – a clear and defined point of attention or activity. It means managing your attention so that it is focused and occupied with immediate experience. You focus your attention on one thing at a time.

Beginner's mind. Rather than responding to events in the same old ways – ways from the past – beginner's mind can help you to see things in a new light. You put aside your beliefs and the conclusions you came to on previous occasions and open yourself up to new possibilities in familiar situations. You are aware of the subtle changes that make what's happening now different from what happened in the past. Noticing something new puts you in the here and now because you are more aware of what's happening right now.

Patience and trust. This aspect of mindfulness is the understanding that things develop in their own time.

It's important to know that these aspects and qualities of mindfulness – acceptance, awareness, beginners mind etc. – are dynamic. That is, although they have distinctive characteristics, each aspect is linked to and interacts with other aspects. So, for example, if you approach a situation with **beginner's mind,** you are likely to be able to **let go** of thoughts, ideas, ways of doing things etc. from the past. This then means that you can **accept** that past events are just that – in the past.

Now that you've learned how and why mindfulness can be beneficial in your life, it's time to make a start on being mindful! The next chapter explains how to be more aware of how you currently use your mind and how your mind uses *you*.

You will see that just by being more aware of your thinking, you are being mindful. And there's further good news; you *can* learn to think in a more open, flexible helpful way. Your mind is up for the challenge!

2
Moving Towards Mindful Thinking

We all like to think that we are open to new ideas and ways of doing things. Certainly, mindfulness and living in the moment is remarkably easy; the hard part is keeping it up over time. Why? Because it's easy to slip back into old ways of thinking and behaving.

To be more mindful, you first need to recognize unhelpful ways of thinking.

Exercise: Thinking in the right direction

Get yourself a pen and a piece of paper. Read all the instructions before writing anything down. At the end of this exercise you will give yourself a score on how well you did.

1. First, write your first name in the upper left corner of this page.
2. Now write your last name in the upper right corner of this page.
3. If your last name begins with a letter from A to M, circle your first name.
4. If your last name begins with a letter from N to Z, circle your last name.
5. Write today's date underneath your first name.

(Continued)

---

6. Write your birthday under your second name.
7. If your birthday is in a month from January to June, draw a SINGLE line under your birthday.
8. If your birthday is in a month from July to December, draw a DOUBLE line under your birthday.

If there is any writing on the page before you read all the instructions, give yourself a ZERO! Go back and read the instructions at the top of the page telling you to read all the instructions before writing anything down.

I teach academic study skills at the University of Sussex. When I run classes on essay writing, I use this exercise to emphasize the need to read and answer the *actual* question. Too often, students answer what they *assume* is the question asked rather than what the question *actually* asked.

Why does this happen? It would appear that their minds are on automatic pilot. In the same way that optical illusions work, your brain reverts to familiar ways of "seeing". When it assumes it knows what it's seeing, or being asked to do, it stops looking for further possibilities.

What's the science behind all this? Well, the core components of the brain are neurons; cells in the nervous system that process and transmit information. Neurons connect to each other to form neural pathways and networks. This means that when you think or do something, your brain activates these neural pathways. Each time you think or behave in a particular way, the more likely your brain will use those neural pathways. These pathways become stronger and stronger. Just like walking through a field of long grass, the more often the path is trodden, the more established the path becomes.

Eventually the pathways become so established that they become habits; habitual ways of doing or thinking. You no longer have to think about what you're doing. You do it mindlessly.

Just like looking both ways before crossing the street; you've done it so often that you don't even have to think about it.

Of course this is helpful – a shortcut to having to think things through every time. Think of the things you do on a daily basis that your brain and body are so used to that they don't even have to think about them – walking, talking, eating, brushing your teeth, driving, texting, etc.

When your brain is exposed to behaviour or thought patterns that it perceives as repeated and unvarying, if your brain is not having to process new information, it reverts to automatic pilot. And because our brains function to a large extent outside your awareness, just like breathing, you're not even aware of how automatic your ways of thinking are.

You become mindless instead of mindful. And before you know it you've fallen into mind traps – habitual ways of thinking and behaving that, like most traps, are easy to fall into.

Mind traps

Being aware of common mind traps is an important first step to becoming more mindful. You'll notice that some of these traps lure you into the future and others trap you in the past.

1. Catastrophizing
2. Jumping to conclusions
3. Tunnel thinking
4. The confirmation trap
5. The conformity trap
6. The sunk costs trap
7. The blame trap

1. Catastrophizing: tormenting yourself with disturbing thoughts about future possibilities and worst case scenarios.

For example, if you know you have to drive to somewhere new, you imagine you'll get horribly lost. If your boss didn't look at you during a meeting, you think you're going to get fired, if you have a mole on your skin that you're convinced will be a malignant *melanoma*.

Worry can be a positive response, preventing you from being reckless, or it can be a spur to action – prompting you to take control of a situation. For example you take a map and the Sat Nav with you on that journey; after the meeting, you ask your boss if there's a problem; you make an appointment to see your doctor to get that mole looked at.

As well as worrying about what you do have some control over, you can also worry about what you have little control over – fear of flying, being caught up in a terrorist attack, being burgled, for example.

The more you worry and play the worst-case scenario over in your mind, the more you strengthen those neural pathways and make that way of thinking your default setting. You are allowing negative possibilities in the future to dominate what's happening in the present.

2. Jumping to conclusions: judging or deciding something before you have all the relevant information or have considered the evidence.

At a meeting, you are introduced to Joel. He comes across as an introverted chap. You know that he is either a librarian or an estate agent. Which one do you think he most probably is?

Were you tempted to think he's a librarian? Why? Is that because you think of estate agents as having outgoing, even over-confident, personalities? It's difficult not to *jump to conclusions*; we're wired for speed that way. Keeping an open mind makes it harder to figure out what's happening. How will you know when you have seen all the evidence? How long are you supposed to wait with an open mind?

Remember, your brain likes to make shortcuts, without you usually being aware of it. But when you jump to conclusions, you are relying on past information or experience to predict a future outcome.

3. Tunnel thinking: Imagine looking down a cardboard tube. What can you see? More importantly, what can't you see? With tunnel thinking, your mind excludes possibilities and options – hence the tunnel. There's only one way to go and that is down and out of the tunnel.

This is useful in a crisis when you need to focus your attention and ignore trivial or superfluous data. But if, for example, you drive somewhere and just focus on getting there, on the destination, what scenery and places of interest are you missing?

OK, in the greater scheme of things, missing scenery and places of interest is not too disastrous. On the other hand, supposing, instead of considering all possibilities and evidence, a doctor trying to diagnose a health problem or a detective considering a crime suspect focused their attention so narrowly?

Tunnel thinking is also related to future-dependent happiness; for some of us, nothing is ever good enough. Do you ever think things such as: "I'll be happy when I get a partner" or "I'll be happy when I get a new job"? Maybe you feel that the home you live in or the garden you have isn't what you want and you're yearning for something bigger and better.

Such a narrow focus can help you work towards a goal. It can, however, prevent you being mindful because you are over-focused on the future to the exclusion of what's happening, your surroundings and what you are feeling and experiencing right now. Focusing your happiness on something in the future means you miss out on happiness now.

Tunnel thinking can also work in reverse – focusing on the past. It might be that you're unable to accept that a relationship didn't work out. Or maybe you didn't get that job/place on a course a while back and, if only you had, your life would be so much better. You're stuck in the past – the past is dominating your present.

4. The confirmation trap: seeking information that supports your existing way of thinking.

Consider this situation: Lauren feels it would be right to exclude Paul – who has recently had mental health difficulties – from being part of a team that will be working on a new project. Just to reassure herself, Lauren calls a colleague who has also excluded Paul, in the expectation that he will confirm her thinking.

It's clear that Lauren has already made a decision (based on the past). She is now looking for evidence that will support her thinking, while avoiding current information that challenges it. (In this case, it turns out that Paul had a breakdown 18 months ago and is now fully recovered.)

Drawing on past experience can help inform decisions, but this is not always helpful. The confirmation trap prevents you from being mindful because you may be misled by out of date information or ideas; unable see things according to current information.

Be aware too, that the confirmation trap is also the basis for prejudice – pre-judging a situation or person based on a fixed opinion or feeling formed beforehand, without full reasoning or knowledge.

5. The conformity trap: falling in with other people's way of thinking.

Do you know the story of the emperor's new clothes? The emperor loved to dress up in fashionable clothes and parade around his kingdom so that people could admire him.

One day, two scoundrels told the emperor that they were expert tailors and could sew a lovely new suit for him. It would be so light and fine that it would seem invisible. Only those who were stupid could not see it. The emperor was excited and ordered the "tailors" to begin their work.

Eventually, the emperor's new suit was ready. He could see nothing but he did not want to appear stupid. He admired the suit and thanked the tailors. He paraded down the street for all to see the new clothes. The people could only see a naked emperor but no one admitted it for fear of being thought stupid.

They foolishly praised the invisible fabric and the colours. The emperor was very happy.

At last, a child cried out, "The emperor is naked!"

Soon everyone began to murmur the same thing and very soon they were all exclaiming, "The emperor is not wearing anything!"

For most of us, questioning what we are told feels rude and intrusive. And, because we are discouraged from questioning what we are told, we suppress the instinct to question our own thinking.

To a greater or lesser extent, we simply accept the beliefs and ways of thinking of other people, even if this produces feelings and behaviours that are self-defeating, even destructive.

Certainly, going along with what everyone else thinks can make social relations run smoothly, but it's easy to become trapped into a single understanding of information; to only see things from one perspective.

6. The sunk costs trap: the time and effort you have already put into a situation and can never get back.

Sunk costs can fool you into sticking with something you would be best off ending, so you continue to put more time, effort or money into someone or something even though it's plainly not doing you any good.

Maybe you're in a new job, but you hate it, it's making you miserable. But because of the changes you made in your life so that you could take up the new job – you've moved home, for example – you refuse to throw in the towel thinking "I've screwed up. It's too late to go back now" and push on in the hope that things will get better.

Sure, you mustn't give up too easily on your commitments, otherwise nothing would get achieved. But refusing to let go means you are allowing the past to dictate the present rather than recognizing that all that matters is what happens from now on.

7. The blame trap: placing all responsibility for something that's gone wrong on someone or something else.

Here's what happened to Melinda: "I'd driven a few miles out of town when I saw it; the red light on the fuel gauge told me I was nearly out of petrol. There wasn't a service station for miles. My next thoughts were of my son: "Why does he *always* drive it until it's nearly empty? Why didn't he fill up when he drove the car last night? He knew I was going to need it today. He's so thoughtless. Why does this sort of thing always happen to me?"

And there she was, in the midst of the blame game. How often have you done something like this where you instantly look for someone to blame for the unfortunate situation you find yourself in? There are no benefits to the blame trap. Once something has already happened, there's often nothing you can do to alter it.

But, because you are unable to accept what has happened, you're also unable to focus and manage what's happening right now. You're trapped in the blame game!

> "The present of things past is memory, the present of things present is sight and the present of things future is expectation. . . . It seems to me that time is nothing else than extension; but extension of what I am not sure – perhaps of the mind itself."
> St Augustine. (Confessions, XI, 20, 26)

Like all traps, mind traps catch you unawares and are difficult to escape from. Much of the time people are mindless; they are unaware when they are in that state of mind because they are "not there" to notice. But once you are aware of them, you'll see that they are not impossible to escape from.

Just being aware of mind traps is mindful. The moment you realize you've been trapped by your thoughts, you are free to step out of that trap.

Exercise: Write a thinking diary

One way to start becoming more aware of your thoughts is to write them down. List all the events, big and small, that happened in the last 24 hours; shopping, cooking, travelling to work or taking children to school, reading a story to your child, watching TV, going for an interview, being in a meeting, writing an email, gardening, playing a sport.

Where was your mind? In the present? Or dwelling in the past or fast forwarding to the future?

Helena kept a thinking diary every day for a week. "I wrote down a variety of things that happened each day. Things like my manager walking past me in the corridor and not acknowledging me (she must be annoyed that I contradicted her in the meeting yesterday). Meeting a friend for coffee (I didn't really take in her news – I was too busy thinking of what I had to do when I got home). Eating a sandwich at my desk while continuing to work (I can't stop for lunch. I've got too much paperwork to catch up on). Running my daughter's Brownie meeting in the evening (why did I commit to doing this every Tuesday evening?).

Keeping a track of my thoughts helped me identify patterns in my thinking. I was surprised at just how often I was letting events in the past and possibilities about the future intrude on what was happening in the present."

Writing it all down might seem a bit much, but the process of writing makes the exercise more effective. This is because it raises your awareness twice: before you write, and while you are writing.

Check in with yourself during the day and ask yourself "Do I know where my mind is?"

You could try this: Set the alarm on your phone to go off at random intervals several times during the day. Each time the alarm goes off, firstly be aware of and then make a note of what you are thinking and what you were doing when the alarm went off. Was your mind on what you were doing?

Whatever and wherever your thoughts, there's no need to judge them as good, bad or wrong; judging your thoughts is another mind trap. Simply be aware of where your mind was at.

Developing the ability to be more present to these mind traps is the first step to break free from them.

Change your mind

Remember, any thought or action creates a neural pathway in the brain. When you develop a habit of a particular way of thinking, it becomes your default setting. So, the more often you have a specific thought or way of thinking, the more you tread that path, the more likely it is to happen again.

The good news is that by using the same process of repetition, you can let go of mindless ways of thinking and establish helpful, mindful ways of thinking.

At some point, you established a way of thinking and behaving and that way of thinking and behaving became automatic. It's a natural consequence of the way your brain works. You can make the most of this process to recreate and establish new ways of thinking and behaving in whatever way you choose.

Leopards may not change their spots, but you're not a leopard and you can change. You can learn to think in a more open, flexible way. Your mind is up for the challenge!

Your amazing mind

Your mind is amazing! Your mind is made up of all your conscious and unconscious mental processes and activities. It can rationalize, reason, think and understand. It perceives, analyzes and judges. It can empathize and sympathize. It is responsible for your willpower, intentions, choices and decisions. Your mind can plan, fantasize, dream and anticipate. It can deceive, worry, remember and forget.

Research has shown that mindfulness can alter the physical structure of our brains. Brain scans revealed that those who practise mindfulness regularly showed increased thickness in parts of the brain that deal with attention and processing sensory input.

In one area of grey matter, the thickening turns out to be more pronounced in older than in younger people. "Our data suggest that meditation practice can promote cortical plasticity in adults in areas important for cognitive and emotional processing and well-being," says Sara Lazar, leader of the study and a psychologist at Harvard Medical School. "The structure of an adult brain can change in response to repeated practice."[3]

Leaving aside degenerative brain disease, your brain never loses the ability to learn and change because it's effectively plastic and constantly rewiring itself. The "magic" of mindfulness is that it rearranges neural networks. And the exciting news is that this ability comes from you; you can direct your mind to use your brain to create itself!

The science

Your brain is made up of three main parts – the reptilian brain, the limbic brain and the neo-cortex – which have developed at different stages of our evolution. Each has an important role.

Your reptilian and limbic brains react to the world around you instinctively without rational thought or reasoning. In fact limbic responses are hard-wired into your system, which makes them difficult to hide. (Just try suppressing a startled response when something makes you jump.) Limbic responses reflect your feelings, attitudes and intentions. Emotions such as fear, guilt, anger and excitement can overwhelm your mind.

The neo-cortex – the new brain – is responsible for your cognitive abilities; thinking, remembering and reasoning, Focus and attention are primarily activities of the neo-cortex. With mindfulness, focused attention stills unrelated neural activity from the limbic brain. Your mind becomes quieter.

Change your thinking

We have already seen that by being more aware of events in your day and of associated (or dissociated) thoughts and feelings, you can begin to identify the thinking traps that get in the way of being mindful.

There are other techniques for training your brain to think differently and helping you on the path to changing your mindset. Changing the things you *do* can change the way you *think*. By changing or breaking even small routines, your brain will be exposed to new stimuli and will create new neural pathways to accommodate changes.

Exercise: Breaking routines

Try the following experiment: Move the clock to a different place in the room. Or move the teabags, jam or cereal to a different cupboard in the kitchen. See how often you automatically look for these items in the place they used to be.

Confusing? Frustrating? Yes. But you can adjust. If you stick with it, after only a couple of weeks you will have adjusted to behaving in a new, different way.

Choosing to break a routine way of doing things on a regular basis can be an effective way to kick-start new more helpful ways of thinking. Even small changes can help.

- Walk or drive a new route to work. Cook a new recipe or eat a different type of food. Take the kids to a different park.

- Read a different newspaper, listen to new music or a different radio station from what you would normally choose.
- Volunteer your time to help people in situations that are completely different from your own. Meet new people. New people bring new thoughts, ideas and perceptions into your life.
- Talk to someone with a different perspective, occupation, background, culture or religion. This will increase the odds that you're introduced to new ways of thinking. (The confirmation and conformation traps are evidence that hanging out with like-minded people simply reinforces your own thoughts and beliefs.)
- Change your mode of travel – walk instead of cycle. Cycle instead of drive. Or get public transport. Take the stairs instead of the lift.

You have to decide to do things differently to experience different results. Write changes on self-sticking notes and place them on the wall above your desk or on the fridge to remind you to do things differently.

Pushing yourself to embrace new activities and experiences that force you to step outside your comfort zone is a good way to train your brain to think in new ways; to be open to new possibilities. In fact, when you think and behave in new, different ways you are embracing another aspect of mindfulness; beginner's mind.

Beginner's mind

Rather than respond to events in the same old ways – ways from the past – beginner's mind can help you to do things differently and see things in a new light.

For example – supposing you have to spend time with a person you have always found difficult to get on with. Imagine meeting them as if for the first time. You know nothing about them so you have no preconceived ideas and no expectations. Next time you're with someone you know well, whether you like them or not, try and see something new about them.

Beginner's mind simply requires you to put aside the beliefs you already have; past impressions, the judgements and conclusions you came to on previous occasions.

Develop the habit of being open to new possibilities and noticing new things in familiar situations. Noticing something new puts you in the here and now because you have a heightened awareness of what's happening right now.

Choose a favourite piece of music. With a beginner's mind you can listen to that music as if for the first time. Pick out an element that you don't usually listen into– the beat, the melody, the lyrics or a particular instrument. Now listen to and follow the music, focusing on the new element you have chosen.

Driving in my car today, I listened to "Abraham Martin and John" sung by Marvin Gaye. Instead of singing along as I usually do, I listened instead to the xylophone. (Listen to this song – you'll easily see what I mean.) The next song on the radio was "Lady Madonna" by the Beatles. Again, instead of singing along to the words, I turned up the base line, listened to and followed that. Despite being so familiar with both these songs, when I listened with a beginner's mind, it was as if I was experiencing the songs for the first time.

Typically, you become mindless because once you think you know something, you stop paying attention to it. You miss so much when you experience things and people in the same old familiar ways. Beginner's mind allows you to take a fresh approach.

Responding to familiar situations, experiences or events in familiar, established ways keeps you out of the present, and living in the past. It doesn't allow you to be aware of any new insights.

Can the same thing be different every time? Yes. Just look at the many paintings of sunflowers that Van Gogh painted.

Or, take a look at Mark Hirsch's photos. In 2011, photographer Mark Hirsch drove by the huge oak tree in southwest Wisconsin for 19 years and never photographed it. Driving with a friend past the tree one day, Hirsch's friend suggested Hirsch try out the camera on his new iPhone 4S.

So Hirsch stopped his truck on the country road they were driving down, and tramped 500 yards through the snow to take his first photo of the tree. Impressed by the image quality, Hirsch decided to make it a project; he took a new photo of the tree every day for almost a year. Look him up on the internet.

Photographer Kelvin Atkins photographs of the same view from the South Downs also shows how the same thing can be different every time: http://www.kelvinatkins.co.uk/galleries/sussex/seasons/

What would it mean if you were able to approach more situations with a beginner's mind? Are there objects, places, people, activities or situations that you tend to experience and respond to in tired old ways?

Recently, I was working with a community organization that was looking at ways to secure more funding in order to continue delivering adult education classes for local people. Emily, one of the staff members made a suggestion. "How about we imagine that our organization has never existed before? Let's put behind us everything we've ever done and the ways we've done it. Instead, let's approach the situation as if it's the first time. Instead of thinking what has and hasn't worked before, let's start from scratch." By taking up Emily's suggestion to think in novel, creative ways, the team were able to come up with a number of new, imaginative ways to find new funding streams.

What new challenges could you create?

Start today: Get used to (to use a well-worn cliché) "thinking outside the box". Approach things from a new perspective.

Looking to notice something new in every situation puts the past behind you and brings you into the present. When you walk into your home, office, a shop, dentists, doctors surgery etc. what do you notice – what do you see? How bright is the room? What can you smell?

Is the journey to work the same in every way to the journey yesterday? What's different? If you see the world with fresh eyes, you'll see that almost everything is different each time; the weather, the pattern of light on the buildings, the faces of the people.

The more new aspects you notice, the more in the moment you are.

Use waiting time – at the traffic lights, in the doctor's waiting room – to notice something new. You will find that you are calmer and more composed with such mindful interludes.

Beginner's mind can help you to slow down, to experience life in the present moment.

Each time you let go of the thoughts of how life should be and enjoy it just as it is, you strengthen important connections in your brain. Each time you look at this moment with curiosity and interest you create new neural pathways. Beginner's mind can transform the way you experience life. It makes life exciting and fresh, it keeps you young and eager to learn.

Actively seeking out new, fresh ways to do things is putting mindful, intentional living into practice.

Doing things differently helps you to think differently. And because it's new, you pay more attention, which means that (and this is important to know) these new activities are intrinsically mindful.

> "If you really want to do something, you'll find a way. If you don't, you'll find an excuse."
> Jim Rohn

All sounds great, doesn't it? Trying out new ways to work, for example, meeting new people and listening to music in new ways. However, it can be harder to do than you think – people often give up and revert back to old ways of thinking and behaving. Why is this?

Think of this tendency to fall back into old, mindless ways of thinking as your thoughts choosing the fast lane on the motorway rather than the more interesting but more difficult to negotiate country roads. Your brain has to build new networks of neurons – memory pathways. Until they are well established, it's tempting to switch to the fast comfortable way of thinking and behaving.

So how do you maintain any changes long enough for a new, more helpful mindset to become an automatic process instead of constant hard work? It might be helpful to understand that research[4] has shown that there are seven stages involved in changing and establishing behaviour. This process is the same for any behaviour change, whether it is, for example, quitting smoking, taking up running or being mindful.

Seven stages of change

1. **Pre-awareness stage.** In this first stage, you are not even aware that you need to or can make any changes to your mindset or behaviour.
2. **Identification and contemplation stage.** At this stage you've recognized that things can be different. You are aware that there may be some benefits of changing, but are not confident about your ability to change.
3. **Preparation stage.** This stage may take some time and may involve several different steps such as:
   - Looking for signs and evidence that you should make changes (for example, "I worry too much")
   - Weighing up the pros and cons ("It'll take time and effort but I'll feel calmer and more in control")
   - Looking for ideas and information about how to behave differently ("I'm reading this book – that's a good start!")
   - Deciding whether the time is right ("Now *is* the time!")
   - Understanding what you need to do ("This book will tell me")

- Formulating specific, positive goals ("I want to be free from worrying about things I have no control over")

In the preparation stage, you intend to make some changes, but first you may be thinking about and looking for signs to confirm that you really do, in fact, need to change your behaviour.

If you understand what you need to do and if you can foresee a possible outcome, you are more likely to move onto the next stage and take action. Also, if you feel that making a change matches your needs, abilities and values, you are more likely to go for a change in behaviour.

At this stage you will need to identify what specific aspects of your life/situation you want to address.

Recognizing, for example, that you want to be more mindful is all very well, but you will need to be more precise. Therefore, one of your goals might be to "I want to be free from worrying about things I have no control over" or "I want to be able to focus on one things at a time – to single task rather than multi-task."

4. **Action stage.** This is the stage where you actually put the changes into place. You change one way of thinking and behaving for another.

The action stage requires time and effort, but with good preparation it can also be an exciting time that results in new ways of thinking and behaving. Depending on the goals and plans you made in the preparation stage, the action stage can occur in small, gradual steps, or it can be a complete life change.

5. **Maintenance.** Here, you will be working on keeping up your new ways of thinking and behaving. You will want to avoid old habits and thinking patterns and you may well be looking for ways to avoid being tempted to revert back to mindless thinking.
6. **Termination.** By this stage you will have established new ways of thinking and behaving. You will have recognized that former problem behaviours are no longer an option. For example, when you're making dinner, you'll stop trying to answer emails or send tweets at the same time. Or perhaps, when your children or partner want to talk to you about something, you'll give them your full attention.

A successful change in thinking or behaviour usually involves moving from one of these seven stages to the next. Each stage is preparation for the next one, so hurrying through or skipping a stage may not be as effective as progressing from one stage to the next.

7. **Progress, change and relapse.** It's important to know that with the seven stages of change, there's the possibility that you will make mistakes and revert back to your old way of thinking and behaving. It's normal and it's to be expected. Understanding that setbacks are normal and to be expected will help prevent difficulties from undermining your determination and confidence.

Do not let a relapse make you give up! Instead, try and identify why it happened. What can you learn from that? What will you do differently from now on?

If you do relapse back to your old ways of behaving and thinking, it is unlikely that you will completely fall back to where you began. Typically, you will take two steps forward and one step backward: making progress and losing ground, learning from mistakes and using what you have learnt to move forward. This is where the concept of beginner's mind is helpful; you open yourself to new possibilities at every twist and turn.

It's entirely possible that you will go through the cycle a number of times before the new way of thinking and behaving becomes established.

Patience and trust are part of the process of being mindful. Know that things develop in their own time. Be patient and kind to yourself; don't think of difficulties as failure, instead think of setbacks as part of the process of change – opportunities to learn, do better next time and build your confidence.

That's why mindfulness is often referred to as a "practice". You get the chance to do it over and over – to create little shifts and changes that evolve into helpful habits.

In this chapter, we've focused on being more aware of how and what you think. The emphasis has been on being open to new ideas and ways of doing things; to let go of unhelpful ways of thinking and establish more helpful, mindful ways of thinking.

In Chapter 3 we turn the focus from thinking to feelings. You will see that thoughts and feelings are inextricably linked – that being mindful of your thoughts leads to being mindful of your emotions. You will also learn that it works both ways – when you approach your emotions in a mindful way, you are more mindful of your thoughts.

3
Mindful Thinking and Feeling

"Begin your own mindful meditation practice. Find a quiet place and then focus your mind on the present moment. Don't think of other things, but sit in silence. Be aware of your thoughts, but be willing to release them and stop thinking about or focusing on them. Begin with ten minutes and meditate daily."

Ten minutes? Seriously?

If you've ever tried to meditate you might feel that that you'll be no good at mindfulness because you cannot "empty" your mind. It feels as though your mind is jumping all over the place and you are constantly having to refocus. Your mind can behave like a new puppy. You tell your puppy to sit and stay, but your puppy immediately runs away, rummages through the kitchen bin, chews up your new shoes, and wees on the carpet.

Your mind is its own entity. It cannot be easily controlled. It's like a television that keeps hopping about or getting stuck between channels. You can't find the remote control so like the TV channel, your mind keeps playing the same scenes over and over again or spends a short time on one thing before jumping to another issue.

If you can focus your mind, then you've found the remote control, trained the puppy.

Your mind *will* wander however. That's its nature. It will fall into traps that take it from being completely in the present; mind traps lure you into the future or trap you in the past.

> "What a liberation to realize that the 'voice in my head' is not who I am. Who am I then? The one who sees that".
> Eckhart Tolle

You've already read in Chapter 2 that just being *aware* of mind traps is being mindful. The next step is to break free from mind traps.

Try to be patient through this process and not judge yourself if you find mind traps arising.

Talking recently to a friend about mindfulness, she told me "I've learned to accept that there are occasions when my mind is more susceptible to wandering or getting trapped compared to others. On those occasions, when I catch my mind wandering, I simply bring it back to what's happening now. I realise that these are the occasions when I have the opportunity to practise pausing and being present amidst what's going on around me."

> "Turn your face to the sun and the shadows fall behind you."
> Maori proverb

Identify your feelings

All mind traps – blaming others, jumping to conclusions, tunnel thinking etc. – come with emotions attached to them; emotions such as worry, anxiety anger, guilt, fear etc.

How are emotions linked to being mindful? First, let's identify what emotions are. Most people would say that emotions and feelings are the same thing. In fact, feelings are just one aspect of an emotion. An emotion, any emotion, has three aspects: thoughts, behaviour and feelings. These thoughts, behaviours and physical feelings *interact* with each other to create an emotion.

Behavioural aspect: This part of an emotion is the external expression of emotion; the things you do or don't do when you experience an emotion. If, for example, you are feeling worried about losing your job, the action you take might be to consult your trade union, or, you might begin to make plans to start your own business. On the other hand, the worry might paralyze you to the extent that you do not do anything!

Cognitive aspect: This aspect of an emotion involves your thoughts. It is the internal part of an emotion – the conscious, subjective aspect of an emotion. If you were worried about losing your job, your thoughts might be along the lines of "I'll never get another job". Or they might be "Great, I'll retrain and do something completely different".

Physical aspect: This part of an emotion is the physical change that occurs in your body when you experience an emotion. When you are anxious, worried or excited, for example, your body releases adrenaline. When you are relaxed and happy, your body releases serotonin. So, depending on your thoughts about the possibility of losing your job, your body will experience a different physical reaction.

There is no specific order in which the aspects of an emotion occur, but any one aspect can affect the others. For example, what you think can affect your physical response. It can also alter how you behave. But it's also the case that how you behave can influence what you think, which, in turn, can affect a physical response.

Being mindful of your emotions

Next time you experience an emotion – for example anger, joy, guilt, pride – try to identify all the different parts of it.

You can start by being aware of any physical signs or sensations: where does the feeling seem to be located? Increased heart rate, a hot flush, sweating, tension in muscles, knots in your stomach, a shiver; these changes intensify the emotion. With a little practice, you can learn to be aware of these signs.

Next, observe your thoughts. When you are feeling guilty, for example, what are you thinking? When you are feeling grateful, what are your thoughts?

Finally, be aware of how you behave. What don't you do? What do you do? What actions do you take?

Just doing this exercise in itself is being mindful. Not only does it help you be more aware of your emotions, it can help you to see how the different parts of emotions are connected, how they interact, and help you understand how they affect you.

The more you are aware of your emotions, the more you can move out of mind traps: those responses that have become a habit and a default position.

All emotions are positive

It's easy to think of emotions in terms of being either positive or negative. In fact, *all* emotions have a positive intent that serves physical and social purposes.

Physical safety value of emotions: Firstly, emotions protect you and help keep you safe. Emotions enable you to react quickly in situations where rational thinking is too slow. In a potentially dangerous situation, you need to react quickly and emotions like fear and surprise help you do just that.

Social value of emotions: Social emotions like trust, gratitude and love enable you to feel emotionally connected and attached to others; **to feel** that you are accepted, appreciated, needed and cared for and that you belong. To feel understood, respected, supported and, where it's relevant, forgiven.

Emotions such as guilt, shame, embarrassment and pride help you to reflect on and adapt the way you behave and relate to others. Trust, for example, leads to sharing and cooperating. Guilt prompts you to put right something you should or shouldn't have done.

Creativity and self-actualization

As well as having a protective and social value, emotions serve your creative needs. Emotions can broaden or narrow experience; provide focus and variety.

There is a close link between emotional experience and creativity. Art, music and literature, for example, can all provoke and inspire emotions and create an emotional connection between the art, music or literature and the viewer, listener or reader. Think, for example, of the way music is used in films to help inspire joy and triumph, sadness and fear.

Often, it can be difficult to be mindful of some emotions because you have learnt to regard them as negative; to be avoided, ignored, dismissed etc. But when you have a clearer understanding of emotions – what they are, why we have them and where they come from – it can be easier to manage them in a mindful way; to allow emotions to *inform* you.

"The past is such a big place."
Neil Young

Past present and future emotions

Another way to understand emotions is to know that emotions are responses to something that happened in the past, is happening in the present, or might happen in the future.

For example, disgust can be a response to something that is happening right now.

Gratitude, although experienced in the present, is a response to something that happened in the past; something that happened an hour ago, a day, a week or even years ago. Guilt, regret and embarrassment are also responses to past events. They can all influence and inform how you think and behave in the present.

In contrast, hope, optimism and excitement are emotions that are experienced in the present but are related to something that is going to happen in the future: tomorrow, next week and next month. Anxiety, fear and vengeance are also responses to future possibilities. Just like emotions that arise from past events, emotions that arise from possible future events also influence how you think and act in the present.

The moment you begin to reflect on an experience you move out of the present and into the past. It is the same when you think of something in the future. Emotions, then, can be seen as movements out of the present, although they are always *experienced* in the present.

Emotions are temporary and short lived. When you are aware of an emotion and what it is telling you, you are being mindful. But too often we get caught up in our emotions, and instead of allowing them to inform and direct us we allow them to overwhelm us and drag us into the past or pull us into the future.

Sadness, for example, is an internalized expression of emotion characterized by feelings of loss and helplessness. The positive intent of sadness is to help a person slow down and adjust to loss. But sadness is a problem when you become trapped in a downward spiral that can lead to depression.

Fear helps you to deal with threatening situations that you suddenly find yourself in – flight or fight. But fear is a problem when you are *trapped* in fear; in a constant state of preparing to fight or flee; stressed and anxious.

Guilt occurs as a result of realizing you've done or are doing something wrong and should prompt you to take action to put things right straight away. Guilt is a problem when you can only keep going back over in your mind, what you did or failed to do; you are trapped in the past.

So, emotions are intended to be quick short messages that motivate you to respond in a way that is helpful. But, when emotions dominate your mind they trap you in the past or future.

Accepting your emotions

How can you stop being trapped in the past or future by your emotions? You start by accepting your emotions.

Accepting your emotions does not require you to analyze what, how and why you feel like you do. It means simply understanding that you do feel like you do, whatever the reason.

Suppose, for example, you've just been let down – a friend cancels at the last moment (again). You feel resentful; you're frustrated and feel taken for granted. You are annoyed that she's "made" you feel like this.

Instead of blaming your friend for how you feel, do yourself a favour by accepting your feelings and saying to yourself, "I've just been let down. Being disappointed and frustrated is normal and natural. It's OK for me to feel this way." Just being aware and observing an emotion can help prevent you from being overwhelmed by it.

To avoid being pulled back and forth, be mindful; by being aware and accepting the thoughts and feelings, you are anchoring yourself back into the present moment.

Accepting an emotion simply means letting the emotion be there; without trying to change the feeling, the experience or the event that prompted it. Whatever you're feeling, acceptance relieves you of needless extra suffering.

It is what it is.

Understanding acceptance

I often use this analogy to help explain the concept of acceptance.

Imagine this: you lose your keys and your mobile phone. You are sure that they must be somewhere in the house, so you start searching. No luck. You try the car; perhaps they fell out of your bag and fell under the seat. They are not there.

You are getting increasingly frustrated. You cannot believe you could have mislaid them.

You call your partner. Have they seen your keys and mobile phone? No. You set off for work, feeling annoyed and confused.

You just cannot accept you could have lost both your keys and your phone. How? Where? Maybe they were stolen? To make matters worse, this is the second mobile phone you've lost in the space of a few months.

Later that evening you search endlessly but with no success. How much is a new phone going to cost? Where is the nearest place to get new keys cut?

The next day you stop dwelling on what could have happened and instead, focus your attention on what to do now. You go and get new keys cut and buy a new phone, thinking, "Well there's one good thing: I got an upgrade on my phone!"

Notice how, in this example, acceptance began once you took action in the present moment. Once you got new keys cut and bought a new phone you were managing the situation – you were moving towards acceptance.

Acceptance can be difficult if you are constantly dwelling on the past or worrying about the future. But the past is gone; the future is not yet here. What exists between past and future is the present moment and it is in the present that acceptance occurs.

When you begin to accept the way things are right now, you can open up new possibilities that didn't appear to exist before.

Acceptance doesn't mean you have to like what's happening. Acceptance requires a sense of realism, an ability to acknowledge the situation and your circumstances as they are actually are right now, rather than how you wish they would be or wish they had been.

What happens next, what you choose to do, has to come out of your understanding of this moment. When you begin to accept the way things are right now, you can open up new possibilities that didn't appear to exist before.

Next time a situation occurs that provokes an emotion, try to identify the emotion you are having. Can you give the emotion you are experiencing a name? Frustration? Jealousy? Shame? Instead of thinking, for example, "It's not fair", a mindful observation might be "Hmm, I am feeling frustration and resentment".' Or, "I'm feeling excluded".

See the emotion for what it is without judging it or attempting to get rid of it.

Rather than judging your emotions as good or bad, (another mind trap) simply feel them and observe them. This is different from denying the emotion or trying to control it and stop feeling like you do; it's simply stepping back for a moment and seeing your emotion from a distance, seeing the emotion as a separate entity.

Accepting your emotions will help you to see the difference between neutral observation and emotional involvement; you simply understand that you do feel this way; this emotion *has* surfaced.

The less you resist what is happening within you emotionally, the more opportunity you have to be present for the experience and see what might be below the surface. You observe and then respond to the message the emotion is sending you in a more mindful way.

Accepting an emotion makes it more likely that you will begin to understand the intention of emotion. Mindfulness helps you to be attuned and responsive to the messages that emotions communicate. Being aware and accepting how you feel and think about a particular situation can help you respond in a mindful way.

It's important to know, though, that whether it takes a day or two to get over losing your keys and phone, or months to get over something more serious, acceptance cannot be rushed. It is part of a process that may involve feelings such as denial, refusal, opposition, fear, regret and guilt.

So remember, *all* emotions have a positive intent; they are quick short messages that motivate you to respond in a way that is helpful.

This is particularly pertinent to the concept of intuition – the insight that comes from the instant understanding of something that is happening right now, at this moment.

Tune in to your intuition

There's nothing mysterious about intuition; intuition is simply being aware of and tuning in to the information your senses are signalling to you; what your ears, eyes, nose, sense of taste, sense of touch and physical sensations are communicating.

Everyone has intuition, but so often it is drowned out by all the other internal and external noise and activity that is going on in and around you. This is where mindfulness can help.

The ability to notice the subtle signals of intuition requires mindfulness; being mindful of thoughts, physical sensations and emotional responses is an important part of recognizing and attending to those signals.

But intuitive messages are often keen and quick which makes them easy to miss or interpret. Here's how to further develop your intuition:

Beginner's mind: Your mind and body are constantly picking up information from the world around you. If you can develop the ability to notice new things in whatever situation you're in, then anything that you are aware of as being overly out of place or unusual you will also recognize because your intuition is warning you.

Listen to your body: Your body gives you information that you may not take much notice of but, if you ignore the messages, you lose out on valuable information that can let you know what is good for you and what isn't.

By being mindful of your physical feelings in everyday situations, when, for example, something doesn't feel right, or you feel unsure about something, makes you more likely to recognize that your body is warning you against something. How, for example, do you feel when you have agreed to do something that you really do not want to do? Do you feel queasy? Tense? Be mindful of those feelings.

Pay attention to the feelings, images and words that come to your mind: Feelings of unease may be signals alerting you to potential problems. Your inner voice telling you "this isn't right" and uneasy mental images also play a part in the way your intuition speaks to you.

Becoming more aware of your emotions and feelings on an everyday basis will serve you well when the crucial messages need to get through, so pay attention!

Ignore distractions: Focus. Once you become aware of your unease and discomfort, don't allow anything else to divert your attention. Listening to intuition is like tuning in to a radio station. You can't hear several stations all at once; you just need to hear one station clearly.

Combination of signals: In any situation, be open to *all* the messages your intuition is communicating. Rather than interpreting a single signal (unless it is overwhelming – for example there's a strong smell of gas or smoke, the other person is very drunk, more than one person is behaving suspiciously around you etc.) be alert for a *combination* of signals. When several signals occur close together this indicates a consistent message; when all the information your senses are receiving adds up, your intuition is coming through loud and clear, so be alert for several signs that all seem to be "saying" the same thing.

Mindful listening

An important part of intuition and mindfulness is the ability to listen.

When was the last time you actually *listened* to the sounds that are taking place around you, rather than just *heard* the sounds? Listening is different from hearing. Hearing is an ability to *perceive* sound. It's a *passive* experience. In contrast, listening is a *conscious* awareness of sound; listening is an *active* experience.

Most of the time you are surrounded by a range of environmental noises, most of which barely register in your awareness. Much like the noise inside your mind, external noises chatter on in the background and form the backdrop to your life.

Stop and notice some of the sounds around you right now; cars passing by, a plane overhead, the sound of someone talking in the next room, the birds outside. Or maybe just the sound of your breathing.

Let the sounds you hear anchor you to the present moment. There's no need to judge what you hear or analyze the sounds, just listen. Stay with the sounds. This is all about being "here and now", nothing more. This simple mindful listening exercise can really open up your awareness to a whole new level of silence within you.

Developing your awareness through mindful listening can help you be more aware of the thoughts, experience and events that are happening in the present moment.

It can also help you interact with other people – to minimize misunderstandings and build empathy. In Part Two we look at mindful listening and see how it helps you to manage situations with other people more effectively.

So far, we've looked at mindful thinking and feelings; you will have learnt how to be more aware and accepting of your thoughts and feelings. You will have discovered the concept of "beginner's mind" and the need to let go of the beliefs and conclusions you came to in the past and to open yourself to new possibilities.

In Chapter 4 we turn our attention to being mindful of what you *do*.

4
Mindful Doing

Our lives are made up of our thoughts, feelings and behaviour. At any one time of the day, you are thinking, feeling or doing. Most times you're doing all three at once!

So far, we have focused on being mindful of thoughts and feelings. Another part of being more mindful involves bringing mindfulness to what you do: to your actions and behaviour.

A good place to start is with your breathing. This might seem a bit odd, but the reason that managing your breathing is an effective mindfulness technique is because your thoughts, feelings and behaviour are interconnected. So, if you manage your breathing – the physical aspect – you will also be managing your thoughts and feelings.

Try it.

Exercise: Mindful breathing

- Stop breathing for five seconds (to "reset" your breath).
- Breathe in slowly, then breathe out *even more slowly*, if necessary, saying to yourself "I am breathing in. I am breathing out".
- Keep doing this and be aware that it's the *out-breath* that will slow everything down.
- As you draw your next breath, be aware of the rise of your chest and/or abdomen on the in-breath and the sensation in your nostrils on the out-breath.

Your breathing can help to slow everything down, bring you into the present moment and give you the chance to be aware of what you think and feel and what you are doing and going to do.

More about breathing

Being aware of your breathing is a simple thing you can do anywhere, anytime to induce mindfulness.

There are a number of ways you can focus on your breath – you can start by being aware that, like the ocean waves, your breaths come and go. Each time you breathe out, you can let go and release your thoughts about the past and future. Just focus on breathing in . . . then breathing out. Certainly, you will notice thoughts arising as you breathe, thoughts about what you have to do tomorrow, or something that happened last week. The thoughts might be pleasant or unpleasant, but whatever form they take, don't try and force them away, just allow them to come and go, without judgement, without feeling you have to give them any attention.

If your thoughts do get the better of you, simply continue to come back to your breathing, which, because it always occurs in the here and now, will draw you into the present.

With mindful breathing, you're living in the moment. Nothing happens next. This is it. You're already there. Focusing on your breathing is an effective way of orienting yourself to the now, not because the breathing itself has some magical property, but because it's always there with you.

There are a number of ways you can practice mindful breathing. Here are three more.

1. Breathing colour: Start by closing your eyes. Then, take a slow, deep breath. You might like to imagine the colour of the air filling not just your lungs but your entire body. Imagine that colour (perhaps a vibrant blue or a bright red?) coursing through your body.

See the colour of your breath expand down the back of each leg, across the soles of your feet and up the front of your legs. Feel it enter your torso and move up your spine where it flows down each arm, around the back of each hand, through your palm and back up your arms to your neck.

2. Breathing and shaking your hands: Breathe in to the count of five. Then, blow out the air in five or six quick huffs (huh-huh-huh-huh-huh) as you pretend to shake the water off your wet hands. Repeat as often as you want to.

3. Alternate nostril breathing: Push one nostril closed with your finger. Take one long breath in through the open nostril, for about five seconds, then pinch that one and let go of the other, breathing out slowly. Repeat alternately. Try to breathe out for as long as possible.

Mindful breathing is like a reset button that you can push to return yourself to the present moment whenever you feel the need. Which breathing technique you use is not as important as just remembering to use one of them!

Just know that by focusing on your breathing, you are bringing your attention inward to the present moment, rather than allowing your mind to get caught up and pulled back into the past or forward into the future.

Try and practise mindful breathing and do it regularly. Spend a few minutes each day doing nothing. It might be before you get dressed in the morning, or before you get ready for bed in the evening. Perhaps there's some time and space at lunchtime? Whenever it is, just sit in silence. Become aware of your thoughts. Focus on your breathing. Notice the world around you. Become comfortable with the silence and stillness. It'll do you a world of good and just takes a few minutes!

Write the word "breathe" on a sticky note. Place the note on your computer, near the phone or on the fridge to remind you to slow down, breathe, and bring yourself into the moment.

In practising mindful breathing, thoughts will still wander in. Memories from the past, problems of the world, worries and hopes for the future will distract you. This is normal. There's no need to judge yourself but simply notice and acknowledge that your mind has wandered off and bring it back to the present. Mindfulness exercises can help you manage these distractions.

Exercise: The park bench

Imagine you are sitting on a park bench. You notice people as they pass you by. In the distance, you can see a group of teenagers on their skateboards. A woman and her small dog walk by. A small child toddles past you, followed by his father. You note their appearance. You observe their behaviour. For as long as they are in front of you, you give them your attention.

You don't think about what they're wearing, don't judge what they're doing nor how they're behaving.

You don't feel the need to invite anyone over to sit down and talk with you. Nor do you need to get up from your bench to join anyone else. You only engage with other people in a detached way; observing them from where you sit. When they move on and are out of your view, you let them go as your attention moves to the next passerby.

This park bench experience is analogous to an exercise that can be done with your thoughts, feelings, physical sensations and observations.

Imagine that the people in the park are your thoughts. You can allow yourself to become aware of your thoughts, feelings, sensations and surroundings. At any point, whatever thought, feeling or sensation presents itself is the person in front of you in the park. Notice it for as long as it is there, then allow it to pass. You do not need to hold onto anything or chase after anything. You are an observer. Just notice it and let it move on.

This exercise can help you to understand how emotions, thoughts and feelings can simply be held in awareness, observed, and allowed to pass.

If it's a thought or emotion that has become so compelling that you can't keep your focus on the breath, shift your attention to the thought or emotion and just patiently watch it without judgement. Thoughts and emotions come and go in the mind in an ever-changing flow. Notice that just as, for example, desire arises or fear arises, desire subsides and fear subsides.

Extending your awareness and acceptance

Now that you are more aware of yourself – your thinking and your feelings – you can bring awareness and acceptance to your surroundings and the activities you do.

Chocolate meditation: A popular exercise for practising mindfulness is chocolate eating. Buy a bar of chocolate – it could be your favourite brand or you try something new – and then follow these steps.

1. Hold the chocolate in your hand. Notice the design of the wrapper and the weight and shape of the chocolate.
2. Unwrap the chocolate slowly, carefully and neatly.
3. Smell the chocolate. Think about the different "notes" you get from the smell – heavy, light, sharp, spicy, sweet, warm, etc. Anything you had not noticed before?
4. Break off a square and place into your mouth and allow it to slowly melt into the warmth of your tongue.
5. Notice how the taste and texture changes from the time you first place the chocolate into your mouth to the time it is completely melted.
6. Take a moment to reflect on, and fully enjoy, the flavour and texture of the chocolate.

Raisin meditation: Raisin meditation is similar way of practising being in the moment. Although raisins don't melt in your mouth the way chocolate does, you can focus more on the appearance of the raisin, the tactile sensations as you handle the raisin, the chewy texture, as well as the sweet taste, as you eat one at a time, very slowly.

Mindful meal: Of the 1000 meals or so you ate in the last year, how many did you eat mindfully? Eat a meal mindfully.

Focus on the sensations you feel not only in your mouth and stomach, but in other areas of your body as well: your hands as you bring the food to your mouth. Be aware of the sounds you hear as you eat, the smell of the food, the taste and the texture.

Think how much time and effort nature, the farmer or fisherman, the food producer the picker, the packer etc. put into producing what you are eating. Make the attention you give what you are eating reflect that time and energy. Eat slowly and notice everything. No reading text of any kind, watching TV, listening to voicemails etc.

Of course, there's no need to eat every meal in a mindful way, but regularly eating a meal mindfully brings you into the present and reminds you that there is no "what next"? This is it.

Everyday activities

Mindfulness is most easily practised by turning everyday activities into opportunities for mindfulness.

Think of the activities that are part of your life in a typical day; having a bath or shower, doing dishes by hand or stacking the dishwasher, folding laundry, cleaning, gardening. These activities need doing – not much can change that – so use them for time to practise mindfulness.

Wash up mindfully. Turn the water on, feel the warmth of the water, the texture of the dish cloth.

Pick up the first plate, and feel its weight in your hands. Use your senses to fully engage with what you are doing; feel, smell, listen to what happens. At some point, your mind will wander and your thoughts will intrude, telling you to get a move on, prompting you to think about all the other things you have to do, worrying about things that happened yesterday, making judgements etc.

Quiet your thoughts by returning to your senses. Feel that mug in your hands, slippery with warm soapy water. Rinse. Repeat.

If cooking and cleaning seem like boring chores to you, try doing them as a form of mindfulness. Engage yourself with those tasks; concentrate, and do them slowly and completely.

What works for doing the dishes, cooking and cleaning, works for gardening, ironing, walking or driving to work.

Try a walking meditation; focus on your breathing. Pay attention to the feel of your shoes on the pavement. What can you see? What can you hear? Be aware and understand the impermanent nature of these processes as they unfold. Notice how your body moves as you walk with your arms swinging back and forth, holding your bag or maybe stuffed into your coat pockets.

What can you spend a few minutes each day doing what you usually hurry through? Brushing your teeth, eating a meal, walking to the bus? Making tea or coffee? Sit and do nothing but breathe and drink your beverage. Doing these things slowly and deliberately you will see how much more in control you are.

Every day, try and take some time to consciously tune in to with your surroundings. Use your senses; hear, taste, feel, smell, see each detail. Don't let time be important.

These activities of your life may seem routine and mundane – getting dressed, cooking, eating, washing, cleaning, gardening, interacting with others, working, driving, etc. but these little things when put together equal your life. This is what you do. And you do all of them in the present.

Each of these everyday activities gives you a little experience. These experiences develop your awareness. From practising these little awarenesses, you can develop a more whole experience of mindfulness itself.

So, make this mindfulness practice a habit. Remember, the more often you do or think something, the more you strengthen the habit, until it becomes automatic. However, if you miss a day without practising mindfulness, be gentle but firm with yourself. Don't let mindfulness be stressful.

Slow down; one thing at a time

Bring your attention to a new level by slowing down whatever you're doing.

Do one thing at a time. Single-task, don't multi-task! When you're filling the kettle, just fill the kettle. When you're eating, just eat. When you're bathing your child, just bathe your child. Don't try to do other things at the same time.

Take heed of the Zen proverb: "When walking, walk. When eating, eat."

Do less. If you fill your day with things to do, you will be spinning from one thing to the next. You will always be trying to get ahead of yourself. Prioritize. Work out what's important, and let go of what's not.

Take your time. If you do less, you can do those things more slowly, more completely and with more concentration. Take your time, and move slowly. Make your actions deliberate, not rushed and random. Slowing down takes practice, but it helps you focus on what you are doing and what is happening.

Make some space. Don't plan things close together — instead, leave room between activities and tasks. This makes your day more flexible, and leaves space in case one thing takes longer than you planned.

The Slow Movement

The Slow Movement shares some common values with mindfulness.

It proposes a slowing down of the pace of life. The Slow Movement began with Carlo Petrini's protest against the opening of a fast food restaurant in Piazza di Spagna, Rome in 1986.

Slow Food www.slowfood.org.uk was founded in 1989 as an antidote to the rise of fast food and fast life. Its aim was to support and defend good food, the enjoyment of eating and a slow pace of life. It then broadened to encompass a wider quality of life and sustainability and environmental issues.

Slow Food developed into other areas, such as Slow Food Kids – an interactive experience for children to experience all five senses and to explore and enjoy food – Citta Slow (Slow Cities) Slow Gardening, Slow Travel, Slow Design, Slow Art, Slow Media and Slow Fashion.

Flow

Slowing down and focusing on one thing at a time, being mindful in your daily activities and routines, all help train your mind to be in the present. But is there a way to keep effortlessly focused for long periods? Something that can give you a real break from everyday concerns, from dwelling on the past and worrying about the future? Yes, there is. It's called "flow".

Flow refers to time spent doing something that keeps you focused and engaged. It involves bringing your complete attention to the present experience.

Have you ever sat down, started a job or activity, and become so absorbed in what you were doing that time passed without your notice? You thought of nothing else; as you concentrated and focused, your awareness merged with the activity and you were "living in the moment". If so, then you achieved that state of mind known as "flow".

Psychology Professor Mihaly Csikszentmihalyi and his colleagues began researching flow during the 1980s and 1990s, after Csikszentmihalyi became intrigued by artists who appeared to lose themselves in their work.

In interviews with Csikszentmihalyi, many described their "flow" experiences using the metaphor of a water current carrying them along.

Csiksczentmihalyi suggests that with flow activities, your brain is fully occupied with one absorbing activity. This makes it difficult for your mind to wander off or for thoughts about the past or future to find their way into your head.

He says that the mind "with nothing to do, begins to follow random patterns, usually stopping to consider something painful or disturbing". However, a mind in a state of flow is so engaged there is no room for undesirable thoughts.

There are eight aspects to a state of flow:

1. Clear goals each step of the way.
2. Immediate feedback – knowing you are doing it properly.
3. A balance between challenge and skills.
4. The merging of action and awareness.
5. No fear of failure.
6. No feeling of self-consciousness.
7. Sense of time distorted.
8. The emphasis is on the experience, not the result.

Goals need to be clearly defined so that you always know your next step. So, for example, if you are following a recipe, you need to have an idea of what the finished dish will look and taste like. If you are training to be an engineer, you need to know what level of skills and qualifications you are aiming for. Or, if you are training for a marathon, you need to know what speed and pace you need to run to successfully complete 26 miles.

With flow, you receive direct and immediate feedback. When you know what you have done well and what you haven't done well, you can seamlessly adjust your behaviour. Taste what you're cooking and you'll know if something needs to be changed or added. Record your running times and you'll know the extent to which you need to improve.

There has to be a balance between challenge and skills; if it's too difficult it will lead to stress and anxiety, if it's too easy it will cause boredom or be done mindlessly.

You feel a sense of control and the activity is so intrinsically rewarding that although the task is challenging, the effort required doesn't seem overwhelming.

Because flow involves developing skill, you are open to new challenges and information so "beginner's mind" is an integral aspect of flow.

As you focus your attention on what's happening and what you're doing, you lose your sense of self. You feel as if your awareness merges with the action you're performing. And yet, how can you be living in the moment if it doesn't appear that you are even aware of the moment? The level of engagement absorbs you so deeply, keeping attention so focused that nothing can distract you. You focus so intensely on what you're doing that you're unaware of time. You are simply living from moment to moment.

There are things you can do to create opportunities for flow; where merging activity and thoughts keep you fully absorbed in the moment.

Here are some ideas to get you started:

- **Play a team sport.** Tennis or football, whatever it is, everything in sport happens in the moment. No time to worry about the last shot because another one is coming right back at you!
- **Yoga, swimming, judo, rock climbing.** Focusing on each individual movement forces the mind to live in that single moment with the body.
- **Sing and dance to music.** Join a choir or dance class, sing and dance along to your favourite tunes in the kitchen. You'll become immersed in the music and really be in the moment.

- **Creative interests.** Gardening, painting, bird watching, juggling, fishing or stamp collecting. Whatever it is, for many people a creative activity is a place to dwell happily in the present moment,
- **Games and puzzles.** Whether it's card and board games, computer games, jigsaws, crosswords or sudoku, all require a level of concentration and provide a challenge that will have you totally absorbed.
- **Books and films.** It could be a gripping thriller, science fiction or a clever comedy. Whatever the genre, as events unfold, you become lost in the story.

Write down the things you enjoy doing; hobbies, sports, interests. They are activities that you experience flow with; they keep you so absorbed that you can't think outside the present.

The more flow activities you have in your life, the more opportunities you will have to be living in the moment. However, it's important to understand there has to be a balance! Too many activities could leave you feeling pressured and stressed.

Gratitude

There will be times when you attach to things and situations that you want, which will make it difficult to be in the present moment. But it's impossible to be mindful when you're dwelling on the past or fixated on the future. Instead of appreciating what you already have, it's easy to focus on what you didn't get and what you think you need.

As the Tibetan saying goes "the moment we are content, we have enough. The problem is that we think the other way round; that we will be content only when we have enough."

Maybe you don't like where you live – you want to move to a bigger house or a better area. Perhaps you resent the fact that you didn't get the promotion you were expecting or that your friend has better holidays than you.

What can release you from your attachment to past failures or future wants? Gratitude.

However small and seemingly insignificant, gratitude happens easily when you notice the small pleasures around you. Start by being aware of and acknowledging the small pleasures in your day and you'll soon be consciously looking for things to appreciate. You can find something to make you smile in the simplest of things, but it helps if you keep your eyes open for them.

Identify three good things that have happened during the day. You might want to write them down in a notebook or you might simply reflect on what those things are, while you're brushing your teeth. Do this before you go to bed every night so, no matter what happened that day, you go to bed happy.

So yes, you missed the train, but, for example, it was a really good cup of coffee that you drank while waiting for the next train, or you met someone you hadn't seen for ages or you didn't have to stand in the rain, the waiting room was nice and warm. No, you didn't get offered the job, but at least they took the trouble to phone and give you feedback, which was helpful. And, thankfully, you had an umbrella in your bag and avoided getting soaked in that downpour on your way home this evening.

Appreciate knowing that you had good in your day, so that whatever any other difficulties, you did in fact have things that made it all worthwhile. And know that thinking like this creates those neural pathways that help to establish mindfulness.

"Life moves pretty fast. If you don't stop and look around once in a while, you could miss it."
Ferris Bueller

As well as being open to what you have to be grateful for – keeping you in the present/being mindful – committing random, spontaneous acts of kindness works the same trick. Opportunities to help others pop up when you are consciously aware of others' needs.

Invite someone who's lonely for dinner, give someone who deserves it a bunch of flowers, make someone in your life a chocolate cake, go out of your way to get some information that you know someone needs.

Gratitude crystallizes mindfulness because when you focus on the events and people in your life that you are thankful for, you raise your awareness of how good you feel right now, in the present moment. It helps put everything in the right perspective and brings you back to living in the moment.

What could you do? Make a difference to someone else's life with an unexpected act of kindness.

Moving on

In Part One of *Mindfulness* you will have learnt to be more aware of how and what you think, feel and do. Throughout, the emphasis has been on being open to new ideas and ways of thinking and doing things; to let go of unhelpful ways of thinking and behaving and establish more mindful ways.

You will have learnt that mindfulness is a dynamic entity; mindfulness has qualities such as patience and trust, focus and engagement, awareness and acceptance, that interact and support each other. You will also have seen that your life is made up of your thoughts, feelings and behaviour. At any one time of the day, you are thinking, feeling and/or doing.

Bring together the aspects of mindfulness with aspects of your life and you have the potential for something quite complex! But not, however, so complicated or intricate as to be hard to understand or put into practice.

Applying any one mindfulness technique to, for example, your thoughts will have a positive impact on your feelings and behaviour. Apply mindfulness to your *feelings* and you will influence the way you think and behave. And if you *behave* mindfully, there will be a positive impact on your thoughts and feelings.

It's a set of simple principles that work together to create a compelling effect; an effect that can make a difference to a wide range of situations in your life.

In Part Two we turn to some of the areas and situations in life where a mindful approach can have a notable effect. Read on!

Putting It into Practice

Now that you have a better understanding of mindfulness – what mindfulness is and how to be more mindful with your thoughts, feelings and behaviour – we turn to particular areas and situations in life where a mindful approach can make a noticeable difference. For each situation, I give you some specific, easy to follow tips and techniques that will really help you to handle things effectively; calmly and with confidence.

Perhaps you have a situation at work; a presentation to give for example, or you've been asked to manage a meeting. Maybe you're hoping to persuade colleagues to take part in a charity fundraiser.

You might want to handle criticism more effectively or know how to shake off guilty feelings about something you should or shouldn't have done.

It might be a more general situation you're struggling with. Perhaps you would like to get to grips with worry and anxiety; stop it overwhelming you and dominating your life so often. Maybe you want to feel more confident, to have more of a focus in life and be more connected to others.

If any of that applies to you, there's a mindful way to approach these situations, and the chapters in Part Two will certainly help.

In Part Two you will see how aspects and principles of mindfulness – awareness, acceptance, patience and trust, focus and engagement, beginner's mind etc. – can be applied and be so helpful in a range of situations

Whether it's at work or with friends and family, you will see how mindfulness can keep you grounded and centred – less pushed by what's going on around you. You will be more able to stay focused and present in the midst of both pleasant and unpleasant experiences.

Throughout Part Two, you are encouraged to open yourself to new ways of thinking and behaving; whether you're struggling to manage criticism, forgive someone or motivate yourself to achieve your goals, there are ideas and suggestions that can help you to let go of anything that limits possibilities.

Start now; turn to a situation that you would like to handle more effectively and follow the ideas and techniques for how to approach the situation in a mindful way.

Make it easy for yourself; in any one situation, don't feel that to be successful, you have to remember to apply each and every mindful step or principle.

It would be stressful – counter-productive even – in an interview, for example, to acknowledge your thoughts, accept your feelings, put them behind you *and* focus on what's happening now with an open mind.

But if you start by applying just one of these principles, you *are* going to make a positive difference.

Because of the dynamic nature of mindfulness, in any one situation you simply need to apply **one** mindful principle or aspect. Whichever aspect that is, it will precipitate, support and reinforce another.

Know that each time you apply just one aspect of mindfulness you are establishing new, more helpful ways of thinking and behaving. You will feel inspired and feel that "yes, I can do this!"

5
Managing Painful Emotions: Anger, Worry and Anxiety, Guilt

The ability to think back on the past and to think about the future means that, amongst other things, you can reminisce about good times and look forward to upcoming events.

But this ability is not always an advantage. Too often, your thoughts can trap you; anger and guilt can trap you in the past, worry and anxiety trap you in the future. But the past is gone and the future isn't here yet.

Certainly, anxiety and worry, anger and guilt are painful difficult emotions but, remember, emotions have a positive intent – even worry, anger and guilt! These emotions are intended to motivate you to put right a perceived wrong. They only become a problem if you let them trap you in the past or push you into the future.

In this chapter, we look at mindful ways to stop anger, worry and anxiety pulling you into the future. We also look at ways to move on from the anger and guilt that keeps you stuck in the past.

You will see how, rather than trying to suppress or battle with them, acknowledging difficult and painful emotions can help you to manage them.

You *can* let go of past beliefs about difficult situations and old ways of handling them.

There *are* ways to let go of your fears and worries about the past and future and free yourself to focus on the present.

There are suggestions here that might be new to you, like giving yourself "worry time", creating a mindful space for your anger, or "acting as if you had chosen it". These are not gimmicks designed to catch your attention. They are ideas and techniques that really do work.

Techniques to leave you free to focus and engage with the present.

Manage anger

Having booked a holiday to Italy, Martine checked her passport and saw that it needed renewing. She spent an hour filling out the form for a new passport and, the next day, drove to the post office 5 miles away for the "Check and Send" service. In the queue next to her was Martine's neighbour, Stephan. Martine happily told him all about her forthcoming trip to Italy. When it was her turn at the counter, Martine handed her form to the assistant at the counter. He read it through but passed it back to Martine telling her that he couldn't accept it as it had been filled in incorrectly. Martine's mood changed instantly. "You're joking. That's ridiculous," Martine exclaimed. She argued with the assistant for a couple of minutes but it was clear he was not going to accept her form. "Thanks for nothing!" she angrily snapped at the assistant. In seconds she had gone from calm and content to angry and rude.

Have you had a similar experience? Any number of things can trigger anger and frustration – a friend does something that hurts your feelings, your company makes a decision that negatively impacts on your work, or someone cuts you up when you're driving your car.

It's not wrong to feel angry – anger is a normal human emotion; it's a natural response to feeling wronged, offended, threatened or attacked in some way.

But whatever your anger is about, it can cause you do things that you will regret. To limit the chances of this happening, try the following mindfulness techniques:

1. Be aware of your warning signs.

In some situations you can feel your anger building, other times you may become angry in an instant. However quickly your anger manifests itself, you need to **be aware of your own, physical warning signs of anger**. Learn to recognize them when they begin.

You might feel:

- your heart is beating faster
- you are breathing more quickly
- your face muscles tighten
- your body is becoming tense
- your voice becomes louder and sharper

There's no need to judge these physical feelings, just be aware of them. Just being aware of these responses is being mindful. It's a good start to slowing everything down and giving you a chance to think more clearly.

Whatever the physical feelings, there's no need to suppress or deny that you're angry; simply acknowledge and take responsibility for how you feel.

For Martine, this meant acknowledging *"I'm* so annoyed" rather than blaming the Post Office assistant for being deliberately difficult.

2. Engage your brain.

It's easy to become irrational and illogical because anger has overwhelmed your rational mind. You need to reduce the possibility of losing control and increase your ability to think more clearly.

So, when you feel yourself getting angry, stop and ask yourself "Am I so angry I can't think clearly"? "Am I so angry I want to lash out, verbally or physically"?

If the answer is yes, then, before you respond, calm yourself down and let the feelings subside so that you can bring yourself back to the moment and are able to think straight. All the time you are fueled by anger your brain is using the amygdala – the emotional, instinctive part of your brain. This shuts down the neo-cortex – the thinking part of your brain.

In order to access the thinking, rational part of your brain you need to calm down the emotional side. This can be very difficult if you feel angry, but it is possible to train yourself to pause before expressing your feelings.

When you become aware of your thoughts you can apply the brakes and bring yourself back to the present moment.

3. Manage the impulse to react immediately.

Slowing down your breathing can help slow your heart rate back to a normal level and help calm you down. So, stop breathing for five seconds (to "reset" your breath) then breathe in slowly for three seconds, then breathe out *even more slowly*. Keep doing this and remember it's the *out-breath* that will slow everything down.

As well as mindful breathing, there are a number of other ways to calm down. It depends on what works for you and what's relevant at the time you are angry. You could try to:

- Force yourself to recite the alphabet in your head.
- Count backwards from 20.
- Remember everything you had to eat and drink yesterday.
- Count "one elephant, two elephants" up to four in your head whilst breathing in, then hold your breath and do the same counting out.

Each of these techniques forces you to engage the thinking part of your brain. Try them; they do work!

4. **Create a mindful space for your anger; it *will* pass.**
   - Go for a walk or run or cycle or any other form of exercise that you enjoy.
   - If you want, let out the need to lash out by hitting a cushion, breaking crockery and/or crying, shouting, screaming or swearing where it will not alarm anyone.
   - Sing along to fast, loud music. This can help you release some of the energy that comes with anger.
   - On the other hand, you might want to listen to calming music – this can help change your mood

and slow your physical and emotional reactions down.

- Do something creative – this can channel your energy and focus towards something else.
- Phone a friend and tell them what happened and how angry you are.

Once you've mindfully managed your anger, you can then think straight and decide what to do next. Don't think for so long though that your anger builds back up again!

5. Respond in an assertive way.

Whatever you decide to do next, do it assertively, rather than aggressively. Expressing your angry feelings in an assertive way makes communication easier and stops tense situations getting out of control.

Here are some things you could try:

- **Ask yourself what you want to happen.** Is it enough just to explain what you are angry about or do you want something to change?
- **Be specific.** For example, say "I feel angry because . . .". Using "I" avoids blaming anyone, and the other person is less likely to feel attacked.
- **Listen to the other person's response.** Really listen. (Use the reflective listening techniques in Chapter 3.) Don't interrupt or start thinking about what you are going to say next. Keep it in the present. Acknowledge the other person's response by repeating or paraphrasing what you heard. Doing this will really help slow the exchange down and give you time to think.

- Treat the other person with the same attention and respect that you want from them. But be prepared for the conversation to go wrong and try to spot when this is happening. If things get too heated, you might want to come back to the conversation another time.

6. Reframe the situation.

It's easy to get caught up in all sorts of thinking about why something should or shouldn't have happened, or fret about all the inconvenience and stress a situation is going to cause.

Your mind will lead you astray while your frustration, anger and resentment intensify, causing more pain than the event that triggered it.

There's a radical way to change this. In the words of Eckhart Tolle: "Whatever the present moment contains, accept it as if you had chosen it. Always work with it, not against it."

What does that mean?

Well, suppose you were driving and someone suddenly pulled out in front of you. You swerve and narrowly avoid a crash. You are furious with the other driver. However, if this had been a computer game, you would've *chosen* a situation that would challenge your driving skills. Instead of getting angry, you would've been pleased with yourself for using your skill to avoid a crash.

In Martine's situation, she had decided to take the passport form to the post office specifically to be checked for mistakes. She had actually chosen this service. The problem was, she had forgotten there was a possibility that the form would not be accepted. If she had remembered, Martine would be far more able to accept the moment *as if she had chosen it.*

It takes some creative thinking – but reframing the situation in this way can transform your ability to manage your anger.

7. Acceptance.

Remember – acceptance occurs when you recognize that what has happened cannot be changed. Nothing could change what Martine had done yesterday; that she had incorrectly completed the passport form. Instead of wasting time being rude to the assistant, it would be more helpful if Martine asked for guidance on what exactly she needed to do to get it right. When you accept what is, you can begin to move forward.

Following these tips won't mean you never get angry, but it should help you manage your anger mindfully and express your anger constructively. A mindful response *can* occur at the same time as an anger reaction, but the outcome will be totally different. You have a choice.

Managing anger in other people

While managing your own anger can be difficult, coping with other people's anger can be frustrating and even frightening.

Anger happens when the expectations and beliefs a person has about a situation and the way things "should" be differ to what actually happens. The person does not see that difference as a good thing! To manage someone else's anger you need to start by knowing what their expectations were. Again, you'll need to use your listening skills.

1. Accept the other person's feelings.

When a person is feeling angry, it's easy for him or her to become irrational and illogical because the anger has overwhelmed their rational mind. So, if you're faced with an angry person, it's as if you are communicating with the emotion, not the person.

However, you do not have to listen to if the other person is being abusive or is scaring you. Say: "I know you're furious about what happened but I'm feeling confused/scared. It might be better if we talk about this later."

2. Listen.

An angry person needs to let it all out, so don't say anything until they have finished venting their feelings. Instead, listen carefully what the other person has to say. You may find that you have made incorrect assumptions about what their anger is all about or that you have missed important details of the situation that provoked their anger.

Do not express your judgements about what should or should not make someone angry. This will only increase the persons' feelings of being misunderstood. The other person has his or her own perceptions and expectations. It is important to try to understand the anger from that person's point of view.

Try to maintain an open outlook; don't jump to conclusions or let your past knowledge and feelings about the person influence your understanding of the situation.

Acknowledge what the other person is saying without interrupting to defend yourself or to disagree. Interrupting in this way just adds fuel to the fire.

3. Respond calmly.

When you *do* respond, lower the pitch of your voice and speak more slowly. This will help to reduce the intensity of the other person's anger. If you were to respond with the same intensity as the other person, you would simply maintain the strength of their rage.

Clarify some of the main points or comments. For example; "Am I right in thinking . . .". And "So, do you feel that . . .".

Then, state how *you* feel and how *you* see the situation. You might disagree with how they see the situation and what they expect. On the other hand, you may agree with their point of view. If their anger is directed at you, apologize and either ask what you can do or suggest what you can do to rectify the situation.

* * * * *

Manage worry and anxiety

The hallmark of anxiety is worry; worry about something that hasn't happened yet and might not even happen at all. Worry, by its very nature, takes you out of the present moment and into the future, allowing negative possibilities to dominate your mind.

Worrying can be helpful when it spurs you to take action and solve a problem, but unrelenting doubts and fears can paralyze you.

Imagine you have a job where you're facing an important deadline. The pressure is on; you're feeling stressed and worry about what will happen if you miss it or, even if you do get it finished on time, whether the end result will be good enough. If, instead of worrying, you simply focus on what can be done right now, in the present moment, then much of the feeling of stress goes away.

Similarly, you might find it difficult to get to sleep at night, because worries seem to loom even larger. It's also easier for thoughts to get out of perspective at night; you're trying to drop off to sleep but there's nothing to distract you from the worries. Nor is it a practical time to do anything about whatever is on your mind. This is where mindful breathing can be effective.

Telling yourself to stop worrying doesn't work, at least not for long. In fact, trying to do so often makes your worries more persistent. Try this: Close your eyes and picture a pink elephant. Once you can see the pink elephant in your mind, stop thinking about it. Whatever you do, for the next five minutes, don't think about pink elephants.

How did you do? Did thoughts of pink elephants keep popping in your brain?

But that doesn't mean there's nothing you can do to manage your worry. You just need to try a different approach.

Mindfulness can put a stop to this spiral of unhelpful thoughts and help you focus on the present moment, rather than pre-living the future.

Try some of the following mindfulness techniques.

1. Accept and acknowledge.

Instead of trying to suppress or battle with negative thoughts, you should simply allow emotions, thoughts and sensations to come and go.

So when you get anxious thoughts and feelings, acknowledge them. Don't try to ignore, fight, or control them. Instead, simply say to yourself "Aha. Worry and anxiety are happening". Think of yourself as an observer, a witness to the moment.

Remember the park bench exercise in Chapter 4? You imagine you're sitting on a park bench watching people passing you. You don't think about what they're wearing, you don't judge what they're doing, nor how they're behaving etc. Do the same with your worries. Let them come into your consciousness and then pass. Just like the people who pass you by on your park bench. Or, imagine your worries as being like clouds moving across the sky. They too come into view and then pass on by.

Acceptance can also help you cope with doubt and uncertainty, particularly if you tend to worry about things you cannot solve easily. For example, you might worry about getting cancer, losing your job or being burgled.

The inability to cope with doubt and uncertainty plays a big part in anxiety and worry.

But fixating and obsessing about worst case scenarios won't keep bad things from happening. It will only keep you from enjoying the good things you have in the present.

So, if you want to stop worrying, start by tackling your need for certainty and immediate answers. Acceptance plays a big part here. Acceptance does not require you to analyze what, how and why you feel like you do. It means simply understanding that you do feel like you do, whatever the reason.

2. Adopt a beginner's mind.

Worry can be influenced by past events and experiences. Going back over and over and reliving those past memories and events can make you worry about the future.

Are you worried that something will turn out badly in the future, the way it did in the past? Maybe, for example, you are concerned that a social gathering or meeting at work was difficult last time so it's bound to be awful this time. Perhaps you are going in to hospital for an operation but had a bad experience last time. Now, you're anxious about the next stay in hospital.

Responding to familiar situations, experiences or events in familiar, established ways keeps you out of the present and living in the past. It doesn't allow you to be aware of any new insights.

"Beginner's mind" allows you to start again; you put aside the beliefs you already have; the concerns and conclusions you came to as a result of past experience.

Instead, think about what you *learned* from that past situation. What did you learn that you can use to make the next experience a better one?

For example, what could you do differently at that social gathering? Maybe bring a friend with you so you don't get left with no one to talk to? Perhaps, with the hospital experience, you have learnt to be clear about what you do and don't want in the way of care and medication; maybe you can even ask a family member or friend to act as an advocate for you?

Being open to new possibilities can reduce worry and anxiety; because when you identify what you can do differently, you reduce uncertainty – one of the characteristics of worry and anxiety.

Look for something new that you can do this time round. Know that you *can* make it different from last time.

3. Empty your head; write it down.

Often, worries are stirred up about events that are quite unlikely but because you are preoccupied with what might happen, you are unable to appreciate this. Try writing down what's troubling you.

Writing down thoughts, fears and worries about future and past events is a good way to empty your mind so that you are free to focus on the present. Keep a pen and paper handy. Then, if you have a specific thought bothering you, you can jot it down, literally observe it, then free yourself for the present.

It's a good idea to go back over what you wrote a few weeks later and see what happened. Events you were dreading so much either didn't happen or, when it came to it, you took action; you actually managed the situation.

4. Focus on what's in your control.

When you feel worried about a situation, don't add to your worries by trying to find the perfect solution. Recognize that worrying and problem solving are two very different things.

Problem solving involves evaluating a situation, coming up with steps to deal with it, and then putting the plan into action, now, in the present. Worrying, on the other hand, rarely leads to solutions. No matter how much time you spend dwelling on worst case scenarios, you're no more prepared to manage them should they actually happen.

Write down all the possible solutions you can think of. Focus on what you *can* change, rather than aspects of the situation that are beyond your control. After you've decided which option to take, make a plan of action. (This is very much like working on your goals – see "Mindful Goals".)

Once you have a plan and start doing something about the problem, you'll feel less worried. This is because you are thinking and acting in the present rather than thinking and worrying about the future.

5. Talking it over.

Talk calmly and reassuringly to yourself, as you would to a friend who is having a hard time. Say an affirmative phrase such as "This, too, shall pass!"

Discussing your worries with someone else can help you to see what your options are or what the solution is. That someone else could be a friend, family member or colleague. (A favourite book of mine to help children understand the importance of sharing worries is *The Huge Bag of Worries* by Virginia Ironside and Frank Rodgers. It's helpful for adults too!)

You may feel the need to talk things over with someone who is not directly involved in your life: a doctor, counsellor or a support group for people in your particular situation.

6. Give yourself worry time, then move on.

Some people find it helpful to set aside time in their day to worry. Then they set their worries aside and move on. They move on to something that they know will distract and fully absorb them; something they enjoy doing that will keep their busy minds ticking over and stop them focusing on their worries. Flow activities do this; they can give you a real break from dwelling on the past and worrying about the future.

Identify activities that you can turn to when you want to switch off from worrying; something that you can dip into for ten minutes or immerse yourself in for an hour. Something that keeps you focused and engaged, that brings your complete attention to the present experience. It could be a riveting novel, a puzzle, a cycle ride or a short yoga sequence, anything that makes it difficult for your mind to wander off or for thoughts about the past or future to find their way into your head.

Remember, a mind in a state of flow is so engaged that there is no room for worrying thoughts.

7. Release tension through exercise and breathing.

Exercise is a good way to help keep worries from overwhelming you because it can change the focus from your mind to your body. It relieves tension and uses up adrenalin. You don't have to go for a long run, or visit the gym. A good, steady walk can be just as effective.

Using mindful exercises and techniques to stay focused on the present is a simple concept, but it takes practice. At first, your mind will probably keep wandering back to your worries.

But, it's important to know that each time you bring yourself back to the present, you're reinforcing a new habit that will help you break free of the cycle of worry and anxiety.

When you're worried or anxious, it's not uncommon for your breathing to be laboured and shallow. It can help to practise breathing techniques as well as doing some regular physical activity to help release this tension.

Exercise: Tension

When anxious thoughts and feelings arise, you might experience a tight sensation in your chest or throat area. It is actually the chest and throat muscles that are tense, but it can make you believe that you're not getting enough air. This can then lead to panic and light-headedness, which only goes to confirm your belief that you are in fact, not getting enough air. Before you know it, a cycle of anxiety begins as one fear feeds off the other. What to do?

Acknowledge and accept it. If you feel that your breathing is too shallow, then allow it to be shallow. The more you can sit with the sensation and not react with fearful thoughts, the better.

(Continued)

Tell yourself that it's fine for the muscle tension to be there – it can stay as long as it likes. It's not a problem, because you are not, in fact, going to stop breathing.

Want to prove that to yourself? You can do this by taking a deep breath and holding it for as long as possible. Of course, you may well feel anxious trying this, because you're already worried about your breathing. But after holding your breath for a short while, you'll be forced to release quickly and breathe in. As you release and gasp for air, imagine you're releasing your fear at the same time.

Repeat the process. Each time, imagine your fear leaving you as you exhale.

Your breathing will, of course, return to normal.

This exercise can help you to feel more confident in your body's ability to breathe. You learn that whatever you do with your breathing, your body is always in charge and always looks after your breathing for you.

Manage your breathing and you are more likely to bring the other aspects of your emotion into the moment. And, because all three aspects of an emotion – your physical response, your thinking and how you behave – are interconnected, if you manage your breathing – the physical aspect – you will also be managing your thoughts and behaviour.

If you find that focusing on your breathing just makes things worse – that whenever you're worried, *whatever* you focus on becomes an issue, then don't think about your breathing at all. Try another mindful technique.

If you practise mindful breathing when you are *not* worried or anxious, you will have established a helpful habit that you can easily draw on when you *are* stressed, worried or anxious.

Focus on what's happening right now

Using mindful exercises and techniques to stay focused on the present is a simple concept but it takes practice.

So when you are about to go into a situation that worries you, such as a doctor's appointment or a job interview, focus on something else. A book that you are currently reading and enjoying, or listen to music on your iPod. If you feel anxious thoughts taking hold, focus on what is happening right now; for example by looking at other people and imagining their lives or by examining your surroundings in detail. Then, each time a worrying thought enters your mind, acknowledge it, let it pass and return to listening to music, people watching or whatever is happening in front of you. If nothing is happening, focus on your breathing.

At first, your mind will probably keep wandering back to your worries. But it's important to know that each time you bring yourself back to the present, you're reinforcing a new habit that will help you break free of the cycle of worry and anxiety.

* * * * *

Managing guilt

After Mishka's father, John, experienced a mild stroke, Mishka persuaded John to move from London to Cornwall to live closer to her. For the first couple of years it all worked well – John made new friends and enjoyed life in a small country town. He often had the grandchildren to stay over when Mishka had to work late. When John had another stroke and a fall, it was clear that he needed a high level of care.

As her eldest son had left home for university, Mishka now had a spare room; she insisted that John move in with her and she would arrange for carers to come and help look after him. It didn't work out. Mishka found it increasingly difficult to manage her father's demands and needs. She became more and more stressed and resentful. In the end, she could no longer cope.

After six months with Mishka, John moved to a nursing home. A month later, he fell and broke a hip and died from complications of hip surgery some weeks later.

"I had a *huge* amount of guilt I was carrying about. I insisted Dad move to Cornwall and then move in with me. I should have been the one to care for him. I just could not. It was impossible."

Carrying guilt around is like hiking up a mountain, picking up rocks and throwing them in your rucksack. Every time you think about what happened, you take a rock out and hit yourself on the head with it. It is unnecessary suffering! It's a heavy weight to carry around; it pulls you down and stops you moving forward.

However, when you give yourself a hard time for your actions or inaction, you're setting up unhelpful ways of thinking that will only serve to drag you down further.

But *not* giving yourself a hard time actually makes a lot of sense for a very practical reason: self-forgiveness allows you to get past your mistake and focus on taking positive action in the present.

Guilt *can* play a positive role in getting you to change your ways. Guilt makes you aware that you have done wrong; you compare how you behaved with how you intended to behave. This knowledge alone can motivate you to put things right and/or change your behaviour.

Whether you feel guilty for eating a whole packet of biscuits, damaging or losing something a friend lent you, or letting down a family member, all too often guilt sucks up your good intentions, drains your energy and causes stress and anxiety.

Research[5] shows that people who forgive themselves for their transgressions tend to do better on the next attempt than people who give themselves a hard time.

In other words, letting go of the guilt helped them fulfil their good intentions so that they wouldn't need to feel guilty in future. Instead of wallowing in the past, the best possible use of guilt is to experience it, accept what happened, learn from it, figure out what needs to be done and move on.

1. Recognise that guilt is a *feeling*.

Be aware that guilt is a *feeling* that you have done wrong. It doesn't necessarily mean that you *have* done something wrong. So start by identifying what, exactly, it is that you think you've done wrong.

Mishka's guilt stemmed from the fact that she hadn't been able to care for her Dad in the last few months and what care she did provide, she felt resentful about.

The next step is to accept responsibility for what happened. So, no you *didn't* . . . and you *haven't* . . . and yes, you *did* fail to. . . .

Mishka had to acknowledge "Yes, I did persuade Dad to move in with me. It was my decision – no one forced me to do that. Yes, I did find caring for him really difficult. I did resent it."

Accepting and taking responsibility is not the same as blaming yourself. Accepting responsibility means understanding what made you make mistakes and taking action to prevent similar errors in the future. Be aware that blaming and punishing yourself does not stop you doing the same thing again because nothing is learned.

So, Mishka's mistake was simply to overestimate her ability to care for and support John after he had the second, more serious stroke. An act done with a positive intention, especially without any self-interest, is not a bad thing.

For Mishka, under those circumstances, she did the best she could and knew how to. She now realizes "it seemed to be the only thing I could do at the time, but with what I know now, I would do things differently".

2. Learn from, rather than dwell on your mistakes.

Just like Mishka, you are human; of course you're going to make mistakes. You are also going to have to accept unpleasant outcomes and accept feelings of guilt and regret. But don't dwell on them. It is important to accept that the past cannot be changed, that what you did is done and what you *didn't* do was *not* done. Wishing otherwise will not fix things.

Once you've pinpointed what went wrong and what you were responsible for **you can think about what you can learn from the situation – what new knowledge will benefit you** *now*. Mishka can't change what happened with her father or ask forgiveness, but she has learnt to know what her limits are not to overcommit herself.

You can try to make amends when this is possible. For example, you can pay for damages or replace something you have borrowed and lost. Often though, the action is over and done with. But, with a "beginner's mind" you can learn from your mistakes and start again. You can empty that rucksack of rocks, stop bashing yourself on the head and begin fresh challenges.

In a nutshell

- Adopt a "beginner's mind" and put aside past beliefs about difficult situations.
- Recognize, accept and acknowledge negative emotions rather than trying to suppress or battle with them.
- Manage the impulse to react immediately; breathe.
- Use assertive techniques to manage anger.
- Let go of your fears and worries about the past and future. Write them down and free yourself to focus on the present.
- Give yourself "worry time" and then move on.
- Accept responsibility for your mistakes and learn from them, rather than blaming yourself.

6
Mindfulness for Self-Esteem: Confidence, Self-Esteem and Loneliness

What does mindfulness have to do with self-esteem? Everything! A key aspect of self-esteem and confidence is how it is influenced by your thoughts, beliefs and ideas about yourself in the past and the future.

If your thoughts about your actions and behaviour in the past (the past could be yesterday, last week or years ago) are positive – for example, pride, gratitude and relief – you probably feel quite good about yourself now. If, though, they are unhappy thoughts and feelings – guilt and regret, for example – you may have low self-esteem and confidence right now.

If your ideas and expectations about yourself in the future are negative; anxious, worried, frightened or hopeless, you may lack confidence and have low self-esteem.

On the other hand, if your ideas about yourself and events in the future are positive – trust and optimism – they can provide inspiration, hope and motivation for future events and what you can achieve. You will feel confident and positive about yourself.

While the reason why a person is lonely or lacks self-esteem and confidence may be different from another person's, the result is often the same; feeling sad, alone and disconnected from others.

Feeling good about yourself and your abilities, feeling connected to others and having a sense of purpose can be easier with mindfulness. There are plenty of tips and ideas here to help.

Mindful confidence

Confidence is not about what you can or can't do, it's what you *think or believe* you can or can't do. For example, you could be confident that you can pass a maths test. You *believe* you can do well. (Whether you do well in the maths test or not is a different matter!)

Self-esteem is related to confidence. Self-esteem is how you *feel* about what you can and can't do and whether you feel good, bad or indifferent about the things you can or cannot do.

If your feelings about your abilities are positive, you probably have good self-esteem. If your feelings about your abilities are negative and make you feel bad about yourself, you probably have low self-esteem.

Here's what happened to Eloise a few years ago:

"I landed a great job as a junior reporter on a fashion magazine. I was concerned though, about fitting in; would I make the right impression? People might think that I didn't have enough experience. I didn't have the right clothes, I wasn't trendy enough. I was full of negative self-talk.

I started spending out on trendy new clothes, went out to expensive clubs, bars and restaurants with my new colleagues.

The bills started mounting up; I wanted to keep up with everyone else at work and so when my cards reached their limit, I signed up for more. Before I knew it, I was £10,000 in debt.

I kept it all a secret and didn't even tell my best friend. When I realized how bad things had got, I felt paralyzed with worry and self-doubt.

I felt guilty and regretful about all that spending over the past two years. I told myself I'd been stupid and pathetic. I was worried and anxious about the future; telling myself the situation was hopeless and I'd never get myself out of this mess.

Things changed when I started to accept what had happened couldn't be changed. But what happened next *was* in my power.

I went to a debt advice service and they helped me work out what my options were.

Once I had a course of action that I could start working on, I felt a huge sense of relief. I felt better immediately; felt more in the present, grounded. I congratulated myself on having got to grips with the situation and I told myself I'd done well to seek help. Even if there were setbacks, I felt confident that I was going to be debt-free at some point in the future."

Banish negative self-talk

How do you feel about "future you"? Can you see possibilities and positive things for your future or is your future negative and difficult? When faced with a new challenge, do you find yourself filled with self-doubt? "I'll never be able to do this", or "I'm not good enough", or "I can't".

How do you feel about "past you"? When you judge yourself in a negative way it can lower your self-esteem. For example, when you've made a mistake, do you tend to judge yourself for it? Does your self-talk include comments such as "How could I be so stupid?" or "I'm hopeless", or "I've screwed up *again*".

This sort of self-talk leads you into mind traps (jumping to conclusions, catastrophizing, tunnel thinking etc.) that undermine your confidence and make you believe that you can't do certain things. Negative self-talk also knocks your self-esteem making you feel bad about yourself.

Mindfulness can increase your awareness of these judgemental thoughts; how unhelpful they are and how bad they make you feel.

Next time you make a mistake or feel that you've screwed up, take a mindful approach. Instead of going back over what happened and spending so much time feeling bad about it, accept that you can't change what you did or didn't do. Know that you *can* influence what happens from now on.

1. **Accept and learn from your mistakes.**

Self-acceptance is an important part of self-esteem and confidence. Some people believe that if they accepted themselves as they are now, they wouldn't make any positive changes to themselves. But feeling so bad about yourself can paralyze you and stop you from making changes.

Whatever you've done or whatever happened – remember that acceptance means recognizing that what has happened cannot be changed. Of course, if you make a mistake or fail, you are probably going to feel bad; you might feel guilty or regretful and that can be the motivation you need to make changes. But feeling bad – guilty, ashamed, embarrassed etc. – is only helpful in the short term. If you feel bad about yourself most of the time, all that does is use up the energy you could have used to make positive changes (see "Managing guilt").

When you stop giving the situation any more unhelpful thoughts, you will have taken the first step towards moving ahead. You can't change what happened but you can change what happens next time.

Think of a time when you made a mistake or failed at something that you felt bad about. What might you have done differently or do differently next time?

2. Beginner's mind.

People with good self-esteem see mistakes and failures as opportunities to learn about themselves. They take a "beginner's mind" approach – putting aside the judgements and conclusions from past behaviour and actions and, instead, thinking about what they've learned from these experiences. You identify new insights and they can help you do things differently, next time.

3. Focus on the things that make you feel good about yourself.

Confidence and self-esteem are based on the issues and areas of your life that are important to you; in the things you enjoy doing and do reasonably well. Those areas could be related to, for example, your work, family, friends, hobbies, sports, interests. They are, in fact, "flow" activities; activities where you feel a sense of control; no fear of failure or feeling of self-consciousness, you know what you're doing and where you're heading.

These activities are intrinsically rewarding and although they might be challenging, the effort required doesn't seem overwhelming. You get immediate feedback – you know what you have and haven't done well, and you adjust what you are doing to accommodate difficulties.

Crucially for your self-esteem and confidence, when you reflect on the activity you feel productive and good about yourself for your part in what happened.

What do you enjoy doing? What is it that is fun and brings you pleasure? Are there activities in your life that bring you a sense of satisfaction, that help you feel calm, centred and connected?

Find what you enjoy doing and do more of it!

* * * * *

Mindfulness to manage loneliness

Loneliness is something that most of us experience from time to time. Divorce, bereavement, illness, disability, discrimination and unemployment are common causes of loneliness. And although moving to a new area, getting a new job or having a baby can be exciting and positive; people often find that new experiences can leave them feeling lonely.

For some people, feelings of loneliness are constant and appear unrelated to external events like divorce, bereavement or becoming a parent.

And it might be a cliché, but it can also be true: it *is* possible to feel lonely in a crowd.

Whatever the circumstances, the common theme here is a feeling of being disconnected. While the circumstances that can cause loneliness may be different, the result is usually the same; you feel sad, alone, and that no one understands.

Is being alone the same as being lonely?

There's a difference between being alone and being lonely. To be alone simply means to be separate, to be on your own. But with loneliness, your mind has turned aloneness – a physical state – into loneliness, an emotional state.

Loneliness is an unhappy feeling of feeling detached, isolated and unconnected. If you are lonely, you are probably feeling you are without friendly, meaningful companionship and support. You may well feel that no one understands you or that they *mis*understand you.

Typically, when you're lonely, your mind shifts to ruminative cycles of the past and future that lend themselves to disconnection, leading to more loneliness. But it *is* possible to manage loneliness; mindfulness can help you to see that a sense of connection is always available to you, regardless of your outside circumstances or internal thoughts.

Learning to be alone

In his book, *Solitude*, psychiatrist Dr Anthony Storr challenges the idea that successful personal relationships are the only key to happiness and feeling connected. He suggests that a person's hobbies and creative interests can also be an important source of stability and contentment.

In Chapter 4 of this book, you will have read Mihaly Csikszentmihalyi's suggestion that the mind "with nothing to do, begins to follow random patterns, usually stopping to consider something painful or disturbing".

However, a mind engaged in flow activities leaves no room for undesirable thoughts. As you focus on what's happening and what you're doing, you lose your sense of self. You can reduce feelings of isolation, and loneliness by creating opportunities for flow; where merging activity and thoughts keep you fully absorbed in the moment.

Don't let yourself wallow. Instead of dwelling on feelings of loneliness, do something!

1. **Explore activities and hobbies.**

Don't be afraid to try new things. New experiences give you something to talk about, which will interest and connect you to other people.

Activities like gardening, reading, drawing, painting and writing, exercise such as yoga, swimming and cycling, can help you to relax and accept a calmer sense of yourself.

They are activities where you experience flow; they will help you feel engaged and connected. Whatever the activity you choose, focus on the pleasure it gives you and the fact that periods of time spent alone *can* be rewarding.

If you have a hobby or passion that you can "lose yourself" in, you will find yourself actually searching out moments when you can be by yourself in order to write, paint, bake, garden, cycle etc.

You will also be able to reach out to others with less of a need and more of an ability to give. You will find you have more interest in them and the world around you, which they will respond to.

2. Make the most of opportunities for social contact.

Connect with others through a shared interest. Consider what you most enjoy doing, whether it's walking in the country, playing chess or singing. Maybe it's an activity like football, tennis or rock climbing.

Learn something new that you can do with other people. Are there new skills or interests you would like to develop? Singing? Playing the ukulele? Joining an evening class at beginners' level will put you on the same footing as everyone else. Don't go with the sole idea of making friends or meeting people. Try to go with no expectations; just see what happens.

3. Make a contribution.

Recently, on the radio I heard a 103 year old woman being asked what her tip was for a happy life. She replied "Give more than you receive. Always do good where you can."

Although, when faced with loneliness, you can feel overwhelmed with your own concerns, if you can help other people, in the process you help yourself.

Experience the good feelings that come from connecting with – and helping – other people.

Even helping just one person is a start. If you're feeling lonely, reach out. Volunteering for a cause or other people will automatically take the focus off you. Volunteering is a good way to not only make yourself feel better about the world but also to help you meet people, other passionate people, with whom you can make a genuine connection.

If you have some spare time, think about whether you could spend a few hours working as a volunteer. It could be a cause you feel strongly about or a group of people whose interests you feel are particularly worth fighting for.

Most organizations, clubs and societies also have a website, so search the internet for groups in your area.

Try to find an activity that offers:

- A role relevant to your interests. It might be to do with the environment and conservation, arts and music, or perhaps families and children.
- An opportunity to use the skills you already have, or will commit you to training yourself.
- Personal contact with the person you help, or at least an emotional connection, such as by phone on a phone hotline. Personal contact increases your understanding and sympathy for the situation of others. Meet the people you help, see their lives and connect with them.
- The opportunity for regular helping. Aim for a couple of hours a week. Frequency of helping is important, because it enables you to build support and empathy for others.

Spirituality

The sense of connection that can be gained from helping other people is also an important aspect of spirituality. Spirituality is about having a sense of being connected to something bigger, more eternal than yourself.

You may get a sense of connection from contemplating a beautiful sunset, or the power of the sea. Gardening or being in the countryside on a regular basis can make you aware of the eternal cycles of nature. Listening to or making music, singing and art can connect you, too.

Being part of a local community or a global organization such as Amnesty International, the Red Cross or the World Wildlife Fund can make you feel part of something worthwhile; something with a shared set of values.

Spirituality also encompasses a sense of flow — the experience of energized focus, full involvement and continuity. In essence, flow is an intrinsic aspect of spirituality. Take, for example, taking part in harmony singing; it is mindful, spiritual and encompasses flow. Harmony singing can provide an experience of inspiration, peace of mind and connection.

Certainly, for some people, spirituality involves a religion – a specific set of beliefs and practices concerning, amongst other things, the cause, nature and purpose of everything in the world and, indeed, the universe.

But for others, spirituality simply involves an awareness of – and relationship with –something that connects you to a purpose in life larger than yourself.

(Continued)

Spirituality is about exploring this idea and understanding that although there are things that are part of the past and the future, you are experiencing them now, in the present.

You can choose to define what that means for you, in whatever way feels most appropriate.

4. Join or start a support group.

When you are struggling with a difficult situation, a situation that leaves you feeling isolated and lonely, a support group can help develop your coping skills and reduce feelings such as fear, resentment and hopelessness that come with loneliness.

Good support groups provide members with a real sense of connection; feeling that you belong and are with people who understand you.

Support groups offer various forms of help, provide opportunities to share experiences and information. Knowing you are not alone can be a real source of strength.

Whether you are struggling to cope with a problem in your life or simply want to get together with like-minded people to develop an interest or promote a cause, being involved with others can help you feel connected.

Most organizations, clubs and societies also have a website, so a search of the internet may prove useful. If there is no support group in your area, for your particular situation, why not start your own?

In a nutshell

- Accept and learn from your mistakes. If you think that you've screwed up, instead of making things worse with negative self-talk, identify what you've learned from the situation.
- Take a "beginner's mind" approach. Put the past behind you and focus on what you could do differently next time.
- Focus on the positive aspects of life; on the things that make you feel good about yourself. Find what you enjoy doing, explore new activities and interests and do them more often!
- Make the most of opportunities for social contact. Connect with others through a shared interest. Whatever you enjoy doing, do it with other people.
- Make a contribution. Experience the good feelings that come from engaging with and helping other people.
- Develop your spirituality. Be aware of what connects you to a purpose in life that is larger and more eternal than yourself.

7
Mindful Motivation: Goals and Willpower

Do you have ideas and plans for the future? Something that you are looking forward to and want to achieve? Maybe you're saving up to visit friends and family in Australia. Perhaps you're hoping to run a marathon, write a novel or start your own business. Maybe you have a project at work that you want to successfully complete or you're aiming for a promotion. Whatever it is, you need clear aims and a focus. You need to identify your goal.

Working towards your goal is not always easy; when the going gets tough – when you face barriers, pitfalls and setbacks – you need something to keep you on track; you need an inner determination that will drive you forward, keep you focused and achieve your intentions and goals. You need willpower, self-control and discipline.

All sounds rather daunting? Not with mindfulness it's not! In this chapter, you will learn how to define your goals and work towards them in ways that will keep you feeling motivated and encouraged.

You will discover a little known fact – that in any one day, we've each only got a limited amount of willpower. All you need to do is use it effectively; to use your willpower mindfully.

Mindfulness techniques can help you to work towards your goals and develop the inner strength and ability to reach those goals. The sky's the limit!

Mindful goals

Remember, you are never in the past or future; you are only ever in the present moment. So if the only thing that exists is the present moment, you might ask what the point is of having goals when goals are for the future? The point is that planning and working towards a goal is something you do in the present. You plan for the future, but live in the present.

Think of a goal and then ask yourself, "How does setting this goal make me feel right now?"

Perhaps your goal is to change your career or visit friends in Australia. Maybe your goal is to be healthier.

If the goal has a purpose that is meaningful to you, then you are more likely to feel inspired and want to take action.

On the other hand, you might be worried about the time it is going to take to achieve your goals. "If I leave my job and retrain for the career I really want, it could take years before I'm back earning what I do now." Or: "If I join the gym now, it could be months before I start to feel the benefits."

Maybe you're waiting for something to happen in the future before you can start working towards your goal now. Are you waiting for:

- The right man or woman to come into your life?
- For a colleague to leave?

- For the children to grow up?
- For someone else to approve?
- For someone to die?
- For someone to change their mind?
- For someone else to do it?

Although events unfold in their own time, simply hoping that future events might occur or worrying that they won't can hold you back and prevent you from working towards your goals. Whether you put a plan into action over the next year or not, that year will pass anyway.

In Chapter 2 I explained how tunnel thinking can lure you into the future at the expense of the present. Certainly, tunnel thinking is useful for small, short-term goals (see "Set your goals at two levels", below) or in a crisis when you need to ignore all other distractions and focus your attention on what lies ahead.

But for longer-term goals, the emphasis is not on *where* you will arrive at, it's on what happens and what you experience *along the way*. The emphasis is more on the experience, rather than the result.

> "A purely outcome orientation can take the joy out of life."
> EJ Langer

It's easy to miss the fact that a large part of the reward is in the journey. Be mindful; see if you can focus your energy and attention on the process – the steps you take – to achieve your goal, rather than the goal itself.

Here are some mindful tips and ideas for setting and achieving your goals.

1. Start by stating each goal as a positive statement.

Set yourself a negative goal such as "stop eating junk" and your mind focuses on the negative words "stop" and "junk". Goals that contain words such as "don't", "mustn't" or "stop" are self-defeating. Instead of thinking "I must stop eating junk", think "I want to be more healthy and slim".

Positive goals direct what to do rather than what not to do. You are more likely to achieve goals that get you what you want, rather than goals that stop you doing something.

Goals that are framed in terms of "mustn't", "can't" or "won't" create doom and gloom and do not motivate you! To increase your chances of achieving any goal, it helps to think of a positive goal with a positive outcome. Your mind will be more willing to accept and move towards a positive goal.

2. Set your goals on two levels.

This is about focusing on both short and long-term goals. First you create your "big picture" of what you want to happen. Maybe it's to be able to complete a 10 km run. Perhaps it's to go to Australia next summer. This is your long-term goal. Then, you break this down into the smaller and smaller steps to get what you want. To run an extra 2 km each month or to save £200 a month towards your trip. These are your short-term goals.

It can be difficult to meet a long-term goal without first using a series of short-term goals. Working on your goals mindfully means that you recognize that there are steps – a process before the outcome. Short-term goals can be achieved in the present. The first short-term goals should be ones you can reasonably be sure you can reach. Later, short-term goals are those that will build on the success of the first goals. Keep adding short-term goals until you achieve your long-term goal.

Have patience and trust – understand that as you work towards your goal, things will develop and unfold in their own time.

3. Think about your goals and record your achievements.

Commit to doing one small thing to further your goal every day (or however often is practical) and your goal will always be part of what's happening now. If you can't do something daily, sticking a picture of your goal on your wall or as your screensaver, or emailing yourself reminders, also help to keep the goal in the moment.

Be aware of and record your achievements, even the small ones. There are a number of ways you could do this; keeping a blog or paper journal for example.

Whatever your goals, record the tasks you've done that relate specifically to those goals. If one of your goals is to run a marathon this year, or write a 45,000 word novel, regularly record how long you trained for, how many words you wrote along with anything else that supports those goals, such as time at the gym or research you did towards the novel.

Look back through your journal or blog and review your progress. It's always nice to look back and see that you've had a productive time working towards your goals, but your review can also help you find room for improvement.

147

If everything's been going well and you've been recording great progress with continual improvement, you can give yourself a pat on the back knowing that you're well on course.

If you haven't written anything for a specific goal, is that a sign that maybe you need to work more towards that goal? Or maybe that goal wasn't as important to you as you first thought and it's time to reassess?

4. Remain flexible.

Be prepared to be flexible and adapt your thinking and your goals. Having goals is important, but when you become overly attached to them, you are stuck with decisions you made in the past.

Beware of the sunk costs trap! Sunk costs can fool you into sticking with something you would be best off ending; you continue to put more time, effort or money into someone or something even though it's plainly not doing you any good.

Your goals may change as time goes on, so adjust them regularly to reflect new knowledge and experience. If a specific goal no longer feels appropriate, then let it go. Acknowledge past decisions and actions, **recognize they were the right decisions and actions then but not for now.**

5. Manage setbacks.

Keep in mind that setbacks can happen. Don't get discouraged and give up. Bring yourself back to the present by identifying what you've learnt from the setback and adjust your goal. All that matters then is what happens from this moment on.

Not sure if you can do it? Feel the fear and do it anyway! You have to take action to feel good about yourself, rather than waiting to feel good about yourself before taking action.

Know that having goals and working towards them is what separates those that do and those that only wish they had!

* * * * *

Mindful willpower

Do you sometimes wish you had more willpower or self-control so that you could achieve the things you declared that you would? We've all got good intentions; maybe you've promised yourself you are going to stop smoking, fill in your tax form or take more exercise?

Willpower gives you an inner determination that drives you forward. It gives you the ability to keep focused and achieve your intentions and goals; to do what you intend to do even when you don't feel like doing it.

Willpower

Why is willpower such a struggle? According to several studies, we all have a limited amount of willpower and it is easily used up.

In an experiment[6] led by Baba Shiv and Alexander Fedorikhin at the University of Iowa, several dozen undergraduates were

(Continued)

---

divided into two groups. One group was told to remember a two-digit number, while the rest were required to remember a seven-digit number.

Each person was then asked to walk down the hall and choose between a piece of chocolate cake or a fruit salad. Those given the seven-digit number to remember were twice as likely to choose the cake than those given the two-digit number.

Professor Shiv suggested that having to remember just five extra numbers took up too much space in the students' brains and so this "brain overload" weakened their willpower.

It's all down to your brain's pre-frontal cortex. This part of your brain is largely responsible for your willpower, but it is also the area that deals with your short-term memory; helping you to solve abstract problems and keep focused. It would appear that it can't do both.

So, when you have to exercise willpower and self-control, in one situation, there is less willpower available to you for other situations, even if those situations are totally different from each other.

Spend the afternoon filling out your tax form or a job application for example, and even though you have every intention to sort through and clear out some cupboards or write that long overdue email to a friend in the USA, your brain doesn't have enough energy left and is too tired to motivate you. Your resolve goes out the window and you give in to eating chocolate in front of the TV for the rest of the evening. You've lost both your will and your power!

Research by Mark Muraven[7] shows that, just like muscle strength, willpower can also be increased and strengthened through suitable "exercise". Muraven showed that by carrying out simple activities that require *small* amounts of self-control you will soon develop the self-control and willpower to tackle the bigger issues.

Set small daily goals that you often avoid doing and get them done no matter what. By working on small tasks that you are reluctant to do, you can develop the ability to tackle the bigger challenges.

Simple activities that require small amounts of willpower

Try one of these everyday for two weeks:

- Are there dishes in the sink that need washing, or does the dishwasher need to emptied? Get up and deal with it now.
- Take the rubbish out each night or make your bed every morning without fail.
- Answer your work emails by the end of the day– even if it's just to email an answer that says "I'll get back to you on this".
- If your job involves working indoors – get outside for a 10-minute walk every lunchtime.
- Only going up a few floors? Don't take the lift, walk up the stairs.
- Get off the tube or bus one stop earlier or park your car 10 minutes from your destination and walk the rest of the way.
- Focus on sitting up straight every day.

Mindfulness techniques can help you to work on those small tasks so you can gain inner strength and develop the ability to fulfil your bigger intentions.

1. Do one thing at a time.

Single-task, don't multi-task! You cannot maintain energy and focus if you are trying to achieve more than one thing at a time. Don't, for example, make yourself wash up, take the rubbish out and pay all your bills online all at once. You'll only overload your brain's limited capacity for attention and get distracted by other things and thoughts about what you need to do. Focus! Do each task slowly and completely. Do each of them in the present.

2. Make some space.

Don't plan things close together; instead, leave room between activities on your schedule. This way, your day is more flexible and leaves space in case one thing takes longer than you planned.

When you focus on doing just one small thing you don't feel like doing, you will start to feel more in control and more positive.

Reflect on having achieved the small task and be aware of how you feel now, in the present moment, for having achieved it. You'll soon find that you can move on to bigger challenges to your willpower and self-control once you become more successful at cracking the small tasks.

"If I can make myself walk up the stairs instead of taking the lift every day – that means I can also make myself go to the gym."

Make this mindfulness practice a habit. Remember, the more often you do or think something, the more you strengthen the habit until it becomes automatic.

3. Recognize unhelpful self-talk.

When you've needed willpower to get on with something, have you said, or thought, any of the following?

- I can't
- I've never been any good at this
- It's too hard
- I'm bound to fail
- I haven't got the time
- I've got too much else to do

Beware these mind traps! As well as doing less and doing it with intent and deliberation, mindfulness also involves acting and behaving without judgement. So beware mind traps and recognize unhelpful self-talk.

Also, aim to replace these thoughts with a corresponding helpful thought. Focus on the benefits, not the difficulties.

Instead of thinking about how hard something is, think about what you will get out of it. For example, rather than think about how you can't be bothered, focus on how good you'll feel when you're done, and how much healthier you'll become if you keep it up. If you have a hard time getting started, imagine you are encouraging a friend who is trying to achieve the same goals that you are. Then, tell yourself those positive words. Phrases such as:

- I can
- I will

- I can do my best
- I can work my way up to doing that
- I can give it a go

4. Aim to see things in a new light.

If, at any point, you fail to do what you intended, you need to do so without condemning yourself. Approach more situations with a beginner's mind; put aside your judgements and beliefs about what you can or can't do.

Responding to familiar situations, experiences or events in familiar established ways keeps you out of the present and living in the past. It doesn't allow you to be aware of any new insights.

Instead, develop the habit of being open to new possibilities.

5. Set yourself up for success.

You can really help yourself by putting things into place that will make it more likely you'll follow through with your good intentions.

I often tell the story about my friend, Sue, who gets the will-power she needs to go swimming twice a week by putting her swimming costume on before she gets dressed. "That way," she says, "I feel so uncomfortable with it on underneath my clothes that I either have to get undressed again, or, head straight for the pool. Of course, I go to the pool."

Willpower to help you resist

Do you need willpower to help you resist something rather than to do something? First, breathe. Breathe mindfully.

Focus on your breathing and you can put some space between your impulses and your actions by taking a one-minute time out to engage in some mindful breathing.

Then, remind yourself of your good intentions. This helps to keep you focused on what matters most and can get you through the moments when your impulses try to take over.

Mindfulness can help give you the willpower to break free from even the most difficult habits.

Surfing the urge

A study at the University of Washington[8] invited smokers who wanted to quit to participate in a study. The aim was to investigate whether mindfulness can help smokers resist cravings.

Each brought with them a pack of cigarettes. Participants were then guided through the basic principles of mindful attention.

They were asked to look at the pack, remove the cellophane then open the pack. They were invited to breathe in and take note of the first smell of the opened pack, to be aware of pulling out a cigarette, holding it, looking at it, and smelling it. To consciously put the cigarette in their mouth, take out a lighter; bring the lighter to the cigarette, but without lighting it. In between each step, the smokers had to take a long pause.

Before, half of the smokers had received brief training in a technique called "surfing the urge".

(*Continued*)

It was explained to the smokers that urges always pass eventually, whether or not you give in to them.

When they felt a strong craving, they should imagine the urge as a wave in the ocean. It would build in intensity, but eventually crash and dissolve. The smokers were to imagine themselves riding the wave, not fighting it but also not giving in to it. They were told to pay close attention to the urge to smoke, without trying to change it or get rid of it; to be aware of thoughts that were going through their mind and what the urge physically felt like.

Before the smokers left, they were *not* asked to cut back on cigarettes, and were not even encouraged to use the surfing-the-urge technique in everyday life.

However, they were asked to keep track of how many cigarettes they smoked each day for the following week, along with their daily mood and urges to smoke.

For the first 24 hours, there was no difference in the number of cigarettes smoked by the two groups. But from the second day, the surfing-the-urge group smoked fewer cigarettes.

By day seven, the control group showed no change, but those surfing the urge had cut back 37%.

You don't need to be a smoker or want to give up smoking to learn the lessons from this research.

What the research shows is that rather than give in to urges, simply being aware of unhelpful urges allows you to acknowledge and accept them for just that; unhelpful urges. You do not have to do anything about those urges, you can choose to simply hold them in awareness without getting attached to them. With patience, you can let them pass. You can "surf the urge".

In a nutshell

- Frame each of your goals as a positive statement. You are more likely to achieve goals that get you what you want than goals that stop you doing something.
- Break down your main goal into short-term goals. Recognize that there are steps – a process before the outcome.
- Acknowledge each small achievement.
- Review your progress. Be prepared to be flexible and adapt your goals. If a specific goal no longer feels appropriate, then let it go. All that matters then is what happens from this moment on.
- Build your willpower; work on small tasks that you are reluctant to do and you will develop the ability to tackle the bigger challenges.
- Do one thing at a time. Single-task, don't multi-task! Do each task deliberately and completely. Do it mindfully.
- Replace negative self-talk with helpful, positive thoughts. Focus on the benefits, not the difficulties.
- Approach situations with a beginner's mind; put aside your judgements and beliefs about what you can or can't do.
- If you feel something pulling you away from your good intentions, "surf the urge".

8
Mindfulness with Others: Listening, Managing Criticism, Forgiving, Persuading and Motivating

Just about every day, most of us interact with other people; people who have different ideas, opinions and needs from ourselves.

For things to run smoothly; there has to be a mutual understanding of what we each mean, feel, need and want; we have to communicate. However, communication is rarely straightforward!

A range of differences between you and other people can create barriers to communication.

No matter how well meaning you are, whether you're trying to tell someone you don't like the way they're behaving, don't agree with them or tell them you want them to do something your way. All too often your good intentions disappear and you can find yourself falling back on all kinds of inappropriate and unhelpful behaviour yourself.

All is not lost! Interactions with other people *can* be handled with confidence and sensitivity.

We will start by learning about mindful listening. This is one of the most direct ways of being mindful. You will see that when you are a mindful listener, you are giving the other person your full attention; you are not distracted by your own thoughts or whatever else is going on around you.

Mindful listening helps to build rapport and empathy, to minimize misunderstandings and confusion; to manage differences and problems between two people.

Mindfulness can help you to develop and maintain good relationships with others.

In this chapter, you will learn mindful ways to win other people round to your way of thinking.

You will also learn how to both give and take criticism and discover how to let go of the resentment, frustration or anger that you feel as a result of someone else's actions.

Mindful listening

When was the last time you actually *listened* to what someone was saying? Actually understood what they were telling you and how they felt?

Too often, we don't listen to other people as well as we could or should. It's easy to be distracted by your own thoughts and concerns, the television, computer, your phone, or something else.

You may think you're listening to the other person, but it's often likely that you are not really giving them your full attention. This is where reflective listening comes in. Reflective listening is mindful listening.

With mindful listening, being aware of verbal and non-verbal cues – body language, facial expressions, volume, tone and utterances – is important. But the real cornerstone of mindful listening is reflective listening.

Use reflective listening techniques

Reflective listening involves reflecting what the other person said but using your own words and phrases. You give your own interpretation and understanding of what the other person said – to confirm you've got the sense and significance.

For example, after the other person had finished speaking you could say: "What I think you're saying is . . . am I right?" "You think that . . .?" "You feel that . . .?"

This can be quite a challenge; while the other person is speaking, you, the listener, have to keep a mental note of the main points or message.

If you've ever stopped someone and asked for directions, you've probably repeated what the other person has told you. This helps you to focus and allows you and the other person to check that you've got it right. It's a clear example of reflective, mindful listening.

In this situation, if you've misunderstood what the other person is saying, he or she can explain some more.

Although reflective listening *can* be used in a wide range of formal and informal relationships and situations; it would be quite unnatural to reflect and paraphrase *every* time someone spoke to you!

With mindful listening, the aim is to listen *as if* you were going to reflect and paraphrase (whether you do so or not). You do not necessarily have to repeat back, summarize or paraphrase what the other person has said. You simply have to listen *as if* you were going to reflect back.

Reflective listening techniques help you to be mindful because they allow you to completely focus on what the other person is saying. Reflective, mindful listening stops you from being distracted and dissuades you from thinking about what you're going to say next.

Try it: listen to someone speak on the radio for a few minutes – a discussion programme or interview for example. Then, turn the radio off and summarize out loud, in your own words, what the other person said.

You can also practise reflective listening with a friend.

One of you talks for two minutes on one of the subjects below. The other person then uses reflective listening techniques. When the speaker has finished speaking, the listener must summarize what the speaker said and felt.

- The strangest dream you ever had
- The best job or holiday you ever had
- The worst job or holiday you ever had
- A pet you once had
- What you'd do if you won a million pounds
- What you like or dislike about Christmas

Your assumptions, emotions, judgements, and beliefs can distort what you hear. Reflective listening can bypass these potential traps.

Because reflective listening requires you to focus, pay attention, accept and acknowledge what the other person is saying, it is intrinsically mindful.

Clarify your understanding

By listening mindfully, you are more likely to notice the gaps in your understanding. You can then ask questions to clarify your understanding.

Reflective, mindful listening makes it more likely you'll ask the right questions at the right time.

Keep in the moment – be sure to give the other person enough time to respond. He or she may need to think before they answer, so don't interpret a pause as an opportunity for you to take over the conversation. Allow silences to keep you both in the moment. Give a person time to think as well as talk!

Be aware of non-verbal communication

Non-verbal communication conveys a person's true feelings and intentions in any given moment. Every shift in a person's inner emotions is communicated through their non-verbal behaviour and this happens in the present.

Be aware whether what someone says matches or is at odds with their non-verbal behaviour.

Be careful though not to interpret one non-verbal signal in isolation from others.

A single intuition signal isn't as reliable as a combination of intuitive signals when it comes to body language, nor is a single gesture or facial expression. Instead, look for a number of verbal and non-verbal communications and actions that occur close together and seem to be "saying" the same thing.

A combination of non-verbal communications is a more reliable indication of meaning than one or two signals in isolation. So be mindful! If you allow yourself to get distracted in any way you may miss crucial non-verbal signs that convey what the other person is really thinking or feeling.

Managing criticism

For many of us, when we're criticized, it's hard not to react instantly; to deny everything, blame someone else, counter attack or storm off in a sulk.

Everything happens so fast that one or both of you loses control and you find yourself unable to listen objectively to the other person's remarks, calmly appraise them, and respond accordingly.

Of course, your response to criticism is dependent on a number of factors, including who is criticizing and why. But whatever and who ever, there is a mindful way to handle criticism.

1. Listen to what the other person is saying.

A criticism gives you an opportunity to practise mindful, reflective listening; an effective technique that helps stop the situation running away from you both.

So, resist the urge to interrupt or defend yourself or do any of those other things that get in the way of really listening.

At this moment, you simply need to understand what the other person is saying; what, exactly, he or she is criticizing you about.

2. Reflect and clarify.

Before you respond to the accusation, check what it is you think the other person has accused you of and what they are feeling. For example; "You're saying that I've not done what I promised I'd do?" or "So you're embarrassed about what I said to Fred?" Take time to recognize the feelings of the critic and you set the space up for a better understanding between you.

If you're still not clear, ask questions to make sure you understand what it is that has made the other person criticize you. For example "I just need to be clear; do you think I did it deliberately?"

3. Respond.

Once you're clear what the criticism is and why the other person is criticizing you, take a moment (breathe!) to think about how you feel, and how you are going to respond. **Learn how to sit with the discomfort of an initial emotional reaction** instead of immediately acting or reacting.

You might want to refute what the other person has said. Maybe you agree fully or partly with him or her. Whatever it is, say it. For example; "I know that you're disappointed and you think I've ignored what you asked me to do, but I do not agree that . . .". Give evidence (not excuses) for your point of view.

If you cannot respond immediately, make an appointment to see that person, phone them up or email them. Start by saying you understand they're not happy or they're upset about something you've done and could they explain.

4. When you can't respond.

What if you've received a criticism and you haven't had an opportunity to respond to the other person? Perhaps the other person has criticized you by phone and then hung up, or someone else has passed on a criticism from someone else.

Don't turn it over and over in your mind. **The more time you spend dwelling on what someone said, the less time you have to do something constructive with it.**

Writing down how you feel can really help. Once you've expressed your thoughts on paper you will literally be able to observe those thoughts.

5. Do not counter attack.

Keep it in the present – do not defend yourself by bringing up offences the other person may have committed in the past. Focus solely on the other person's grievance. (Once you've resolved this situation – *then* you can say "Now that we've sorted that out, I'd like to talk about . . .".)

6. Repeat the process.

Listen to the other person's response and continue the process; listening, acknowledging and responding.

7. Agree to disagree.

If you can resolve the situation, all well and good. But if not, learn when to draw a line and agree to disagree.

8. Look for seeds of truth in criticism.

Criticism opens you up to new perspectives and new ideas that you may not have considered before. It's not easy to take an honest look at yourself and your weaknesses. Again, **learn how to sit with the discomfort of an initial emotional reaction** instead of immediately acting or reacting.

You might disagree with the other person. Fine. But is there something to be learnt from the situation, now, in the present moment?

9. Don't sweat the small stuff!

Get things into perspective; does it really matter that your partner thinks you load the dishwasher all "wrong"? You can't please all the people all the time; it can be liberating to let people think whatever they want – they're going to do it anyway. Accept it. Then let it go!

Giving criticism
Receiving criticism is the hard part, right? Giving criticism is easy.

Actually, no. Giving someone criticism in a clear, calm and honest way is rarely easy.

Some people confront the problem head on. Others hold back their criticism; they don't want to cause any unpleasantness but, instead, build resentment with all that's been unsaid.

Of course the other person may react badly to criticism, but this doesn't mean that you should shy away from what you want to say. There are two key steps you should go through when you find yourself in this position:

1. Before you say anything, decide what, exactly, it is that the other person has done that's a problem for you.
2. Decide what change you want to see; what you want them to do or say next.

For example, imagine you are annoyed with Anya; in a meeting at work this morning, she ridiculed Fred for finding it difficult to explain how he planned to implement a new strategy.

Why are you going to criticize Anya? What's your intention? Do you just want to get it off your chest so that you can feel better? Do you want to humiliate her in the same way that she humiliated Fred? Or maybe you are intending to be more constructive than that; you want to make her aware of how hurt Fred is and suggest she apologizes to Fred.

An old Arab proverb suggests three gates you should be able to pass through before you open your mouth to speak: Is it necessary? Is it kind? Is it true?

Your criticism should be able to pass through at least two of these gates. So, telling Anya that she's a self-centred bitch might be true, but it will never pass the "necessary" or "kind" gates!

The following tips can help you pass through these three gates smoothly and ensure that when you need to give criticism, you do so in a calm and honest way.

1. Consider the time and place.

Do you have to say something immediately, or can it wait until the other person is more likely to listen to you? If you can, choose the time and the place. Although it is best to say something immediately, it may not be appropriate – particularly if there are other people around. Give criticism to the other person directly, and if at all possible, face to face. But never on Facebook! Show respect.

Although you may have to wait for an appropriate time and place, don't let things build up to such an extent that they just get worse. Tackle it as soon as possible. The consequence of ignoring the other person's behaviour will just be detrimental to you both.

2. Focus on one thing at a time.

If you have more than one issue, focus on one problem at a time and deal with the most important issue first.

Keep it in the present. Don't bring up past misdemeanors or allow yourself to be dragged into other issues by the other person either.

3. Focus on the action, not the individual.

This is not an opportunity to dissect the other person's every mistake and character flaw for the past two years. Focus on your specific concern and keep it brief – avoid going on and on long after you have made your point.

4. Do not accuse and judge.

Do not tell the other person "*You* do this and *you* do that". "You" messages label the other person in a negative way.

Instead, use "I" statements. So, instead of saying to your friend "You need to stop laughing at people when they make a mistake" say "I didn't like it when you laughed at Fred when he made a mistake".

5. Tell the other person how you feel.

Are you jealous, angry, upset? Say so. Don't be afraid to tell the other person how you feel: "I was upset/embarrassed/furious when . . .".

6. Listen to the other person's response.

Listen mindfully. Do not interrupt; there is a chance the other person may give you some information that you didn't know and which changes your view. Check this by repeating what they say, "Have I got this right? You're saying that . . .".

7. Decide what your next step will be.

If the other person doesn't do what you want, what will you do? This doesn't mean issuing threats or punishments. It means deciding what your next step will be. You have a choice: you can either stick to what you want and decide what will happen if you don't get it. Or, you can negotiate or compromise. Or you can rest assured that you have made your point, accept that the other person does not agree; let go and move on.

* * * * *

Mindful forgiveness

"Forgiveness does not change the past, but it does enlarge the future."
Paul Boese

Has someone ever pushed in front of you – on purpose or inadvertently – when you were in a queue at the cinema or supermarket? Did a friend once spill red wine on your sofa? Did you ever get to your local shop and discover it had sold out of newspapers or milk?

Did you manage to forgive and forget? Most probably!

Of course, minor offences such as someone pushing in front of you, knocking a glass of wine over or the shop selling out of milk are easy to forgive and forget. But what if you are faced with more serious issues? What if your partner has had an affair, you've been unfairly sacked or you've received an injury as a result of someone else's actions? It can be a real struggle to accept what happened and forgive the other person or people involved.

Forgiveness means letting go of the resentment, frustration or anger that you feel as a result of someone else's actions. It involves no longer wanting punishment, revenge or compensation.

If you have reached a point where you do want to put it all behind you and move on with your life, then mindfulness can help by going through the following three stages.

1. Be aware of how and what you feel.

Start by being aware of how and what you feel. Angry, upset, disappointed? Jealous or resentful? All of the above? That's ok. Give yourself permission to feel the emotions and process them. The less you resist what is happening within you emotionally, the more opportunity you have to be mindful about the situation.

See if you can tease apart the difference between your feelings about what happened and your feelings for the person who did you wrong.

Maybe you're angry and upset about what happened. Perhaps you even feel you could have done something to prevent what happened.

You may find it difficult to forgive the other person because you are suffering and so you want the other person to suffer too; to be punished. You refuse to forgive them because you fear it will make you vulnerable again. You want to protect yourself and take control.

Be aware though, that not forgiving someone will not ensure you won't be hurt again, and forgiving someone won't mean that you will be.

2. Allow yourself to let go.

It might help if you understand that all the time you don't forgive, you are tied to the other person or event. Forgiveness allows you to free yourself from the other person, the event and all associated suffering. When you let go of your need to punish the other person you can move forward.

> "Letting go is the natural release which always follows the realization that holding on is an energy drain and it hurts."
> Larry James

Forgiving doesn't mean giving in. If the other person has not apologized, or has apologized only to repeat the offence, nothing requires you to trust him or her. While there's no point in tormenting yourself over this person's actions, you do not need to fall victim to their actions again.

3. Accept what has happened.

Know that forgiveness flows from acceptance. You cannot change what has already happened. It is what it is. But how many times a day do you think about this hurt? How many times have you told the story about how badly you were wronged? Know that every time you think about it or retell the story to other people you are back in the past.

Holding on to your resentment keeps you in the past; a place where you have no influence. When you can accept that what has happened, happened in the past, then you are on the road to forgiveness.

In an interview with Time magazine,[9] 30 years after her husband was murdered, Yoko Ono was asked; "Can you forgive John Lennon's murderer, Mark Chapman?" She replied, "I have not been able to forgive him yet. But I'm not thinking about him all the time. And that's good."

Certainly, the other person is responsible for his or her actions; he or she may not deserve to be forgiven for your pain, sadness and suffering but *you* deserve to be free of this negativity. Forgiveness is for you and not the other person!

Realize that the hate, anger or bitterness you feel towards the other person has little or no effect on him or her; they are probably just getting on with their life.

"Resentment is like drinking poison and waiting for it to kill your enemy."
Nelson Mandela

4. Learn from what happened and move on.

Letting go of what cannot be changed allows you to move into the present and look forward rather than backwards. Open yourself to new possibilities.

Think of the positive things that emerged as a result of the experience. You've dwelt long enough on the bad, hurtful aspects of what happened. Now focus on the positive side. This is the key to transforming what happened.

Think back, for example, to anyone who might have helped and supported you. Focus your thoughts on their kindness and selflessness. Thinking in this way; directing your mind to the positive aspects of the event prevents angry, bitter, resentful thoughts from continuing.

Be kind to yourself. Give yourself *time* to heal. Know that letting go, acceptance and forgiveness are all part of a process. Sometimes your ability to forgive will come quickly and easily. At other times and in other circumstances you may find that healing and forgiveness take months, or even years.

"Letting go is a journey that never ends."
Larry James

Forgiveness is not always a once-and-done event. You may be faced with the memory of something long after you have forgiven and forgotten. Those feelings you had when it first happened might coming rushing back. That's ok. It doesn't mean that your efforts at forgiveness were a waste of time. It simply means you've had a painful memory resurface.

If you suddenly find yourself confronted by painful memories, accepting and acknowledging how you feel, grounding yourself with, for example, mindful breathing can help you to manage the moment.

* * * * *

Mindfulness to persuade others

People who are mindful when motivating, persuading and influencing others, tend to be effective in understanding and relating to others, and are able to motivate them toward shared goals. They know that the way to get other people on their side is to be very clear about what they want, to choose the right time to talk to the other person, to present their suggestion as an attractive way forward and to be able to negotiate and compromise.

Whether you are hoping to persuade your partner to cook dinner this evening or motivate colleagues to take part in a charity fundraiser, there are mindful ways to do it.

Make an unusual request
Elaine was hoping to persuade her colleagues to take part in a fundraising event. She suggested a sponsored walk, but only one or two people showed any interest. The others just glazed over at Elaine's suggestion.

Elaine got a completely different response when she suggested "Indian Bingo" as a fundraiser. Her colleagues were intrigued; they were keen to know what, exactly, "Indian Bingo" was!

According to research, when people are asked something that's a typical, regular or routine request, whether they agree or disagree, they will respond mindlessly.

A study by Santos et al. 2006[10] in the USA showed that people are more easily persuaded if their awareness is raised by an *unusual* request.

Passers-by were approached by a person who made an unusual request – "Can you spare 17 cents (or 37 cents)?" – or made a typical request – "Can you spare a quarter (or any change)?" People subjected to the unusual request were 60% more likely to give money than those receiving the typical plea. The strange request provoked increased interest as evidenced by the number of verbal inquiries about the request.

So, when you are hoping to persuade and motivate someone, ask yourself what you already know about the other person that might help you to engage him or her. What might catch their interest?

Are you relying on past knowledge of the other person? Rather than relying on the usual ways of persuading and motivating others, try a new approach. Know that mindlessness turns to mindfulness when awareness is heightened.

Ask yourself what are *their* interests and goals? What will attract their attention? And be sure to choose a good time so you can *persuade* the other person when they are at their most responsive, not when they are tired stressed or likely to be distracted.

Whether your request is typical or unusual, make sure you know what, exactly, it is that you want to persuade the other person to do. Keep it focused; simplify your request and don't ramble on, otherwise your message will be lost.

When you are trying to persuade someone to do something, tell them how it will benefit them. It's important to be genuine and sincere. For example "if you cook dinner tonight, then I can finish this work, put the children to bed and that will leave enough time for us both to watch that film on DVD". Do, though, keep in mind that persuasion should use suggestion not demand.

Listen and acknowledge the other person

Listen to the response. Be a good listener and take the other person's point of view into consideration. People are far more willing to cooperate if they feel acknowledged, understood and appreciated.

Ask questions. What are their concerns? Acknowledge and address those needs and concerns. **Use positive, rather than negative language:** instead of saying "You're wrong about this", say "I understand that you think /feel that, but . . .", or "I agree with what you say on. . . . but have you considered . . .".

Know when to **compromise**, but also know when to accept that other people are not going to come round to your way of thinking. Let it go – give up trying to persuade and, instead, formulate a plan B!

In a nutshell

- Always listen *as if* you were going to reflect back what the other person said. You do not necessarily have to repeat back what the other person has said. You simply have to listen *as if* you are going to reflect back.
- If you are on the receiving end of criticism, instead of rushing straight into an argument, learn how to sit with the discomfort of the initial emotional reaction.

- Use mindful listening skills. Resist the urge to interrupt or defend yourself. Listen, reflect and clarify. Then respond.
- If you are *giving* criticism, focus on one problem at a time. Keep it in the present. Don't bring up past complaints or get dragged into other issues.
- If you can resolve the situation, all well and good. But if not, learn when to draw a line and agree to disagree.
- Forgive and forget. Learn from what happened and move on. Know that letting go, acceptance and forgiveness are all part of the process.
- To persuade others, be clear about what you want, choose a good time and present your suggestion as an attractive way forward.
- In all situations, know when to negotiate and compromise.

9
Mindfulness at Work: Interviews, Meetings and Presentations

"How's work"? For many people, a typical answer is "Stressful. My manager is a nightmare – she calls meeting after meeting but no real decisions are ever made. I've got a presentation to do tomorrow which I'm dreading. I'm looking for another job. I've got an interview next week which I'm nervous about."

Too often, when you are faced with pressures and responsibilities at work, a current of negative thoughts and feelings can sweep you along. When this happens, it's not easy to think straight, do your job well and enjoy it.

Mindfulness can help. It can keep you grounded and centred – less pushed by what's going on around you. You are more able to stay focused and be calmly present in the midst of both pleasant and unpleasant situations at work.

You can be more flexible with your thinking and let go of established ways of working. You *can* develop a stronger self belief; you *can* be positive about your abilities.

A mindful approach helps you to work with other people more effectively. You are more aware of other people's needs and feelings; you are able to understand another person's ideas and suggestions from their perspective.

Being mindful at work does not prevent conflict from arising or difficult issues from coming up. But when problems do arise, a mindful approach can help you manage difficult, trying and stressful situations with more confidence and ease. You are more accepting of other people and the differences between you.

In this chapter, we look at specific situations – interviews, meetings and presentations and explain how to manage them mindfully.

Mindfulness for interviews

Getting an interview is an achievement in itself; not everyone who applied for the same job as you was invited for an interview. But, for many people, the pleasure of being invited for an interview can quickly turn to worry and anxiety. Thoughts such as "I might not understand what they ask me", or "I'll talk too quickly", quickly find their way into your head.

Then, on the day of the interview you arrive with a dry mouth, your palms are sweaty and you can hear your heart thumping.

It doesn't need to be like that!

1. Put past interviews behind you.

Don't go over job interviews that didn't go well. This is a different job with a different interviewer. If you learnt anything useful from the last interview, all well and good. Otherwise, put it behind you, open yourself to new possibilities and focus on *this* interview, now.

2. Prepare yourself.

All the usual advice about being prepared applies, so do your research. Research the potential employer's services, markets and their competitors. Plan what you'll wear and make sure you know where you're going and how to get there. Don't forget to leave enough spare time for transport delays.

On the day before the interview, read your application form again. Some of the questions you will be asked will arise from what you have written in your application. You need to remember what you have written! Being prepared will help ease the tension that the unknown brings and make you feel more confident.

3. Plan to relax.

The evening before the interview, do something that you know will engage and absorb you. Watch a film, meet up with friends – do anything that you enjoy, that will engage your attention and make it difficult for worries about the interview to find their way into your head.

4. Breathe.

Just before the interview, while you're waiting to be called in, calm yourself. Breathe! Use one of the breathing techniques in Chapter 4.

You could also try this: imagine a smile on the face of someone you love – you might find it easier to visualize or you can bring a photograph of them with you. Respond with a smile of your own and you will look calm and relaxed when you arrive in the interview.

5. **Listen.**

Don't let your thoughts influence how well you listen. Wait until the interviewer has finished asking the question and *then* respond. If you need a minute to think, say so. If you are uncertain what the interviewer is asking you, say so. This approach will show that you will have the confidence to pause and think and/or seek clarification in the job if and when it's necessary. If you don't know the answer to a question, say so. Never lie.

Answer the questions in a confident, firm voice. Try not to mumble or rush.

6. **Let go.**

After the interview, don't spend the rest of the day going back over things you wish you had or hadn't said. Instead, plan to do something you'll enjoy; meet a friend for lunch or play a game of tennis for example.

Whether you get the job or not, ask for feedback on how you did in the interview. Honest feedback means that you can go on to improve your interview style by working on the areas you didn't do so well in. By doing this, you've moved on and started preparing for the next interview.

Using mindfulness to give stronger presentations

Does the thought of speaking in front of a group of people make you go weak at the knees? Whether it's giving a speech at a social occasion or at a business presentation, many people find public speaking terrifying.

"I'm sure I'll leave out something important", "I'll talk too quickly", "I'll mumble", "They'll all know I'm nervous", "I'll know, just by looking at their faces, that people are bored".

Getting caught up in images and feelings in your mind that create anxiety will undermine your confidence. And yet, confidence is exactly what you need; you need to believe that you can do it.

1. Be better prepared.

It goes without saying that you should plan what to say and in what order to say it.

If you know your topic well, you're more than halfway there. Why? Because if you know *what* you are going to say, then when you're giving the talk, you can simply focus on *how* you say it and engaging the audience rather than jumping ahead of yourself and worrying that you're going to forget something.

So, you should decide first what the main message of your talk is and second, what the main points that you want to make are.

You should also rehearse your presentation – to yourself first and then in front of a friend or colleague. Ask for honest feedback – what is good and what can be improved?

Managing your thoughts is just as important as rehearsing. If you make a mistake in the rehearsal, for example you forget to include an important point, instead of catastrophizing – "Oh that was awful, I'll never be able to do this presentation properly" – think of ways to get round the problem.

2. Breathe!

The most fearful moments of any presentation are the few minutes before your stage entrance. Avoid tormenting yourself with unhelpful thoughts. Instead, use positive self-talk: "I can do this. It will be fine". Breathe. Use a breathing technique that works for you.

Never read from a script. This might help avoid hesitations and rambling deviations but it's difficult to communicate well with your audience if your head is stuck in a piece of paper! There's no need to memorize your entire speech or presentation word for word. The real pros deliver their material by writing down key points, sub topics and examples to cover on prompt cards.

If you are using PowerPoint slides, these can serve as your prompts and as a guide for the audience. But too many presentations and speeches are boring monologues filled with endless PowerPoint slides. A monologue, where you do all the talking and/or everyone stares at the screen, puts all the responsibility for informing and entertaining the audience on you.

3. Actively engage your audience.

Engage your audience – ask them questions and find other ways to get them to participate. This will stop their minds from wandering and keep them focused. Having the group involved paces the presentation, keeps it in the moment, stops you rushing ahead. It also gives you time to reorganize your thoughts if things are going off track.

Keep to the time allowed but avoid rushing through your presentation; try to speak fairly slowly and pause after each key point. Pausing at the end of key points helps to emphasize each separate point you are making. Listen to Barack Obama – he does this very effectively.

Stick to the plan for the presentation, don't be tempted to digress – you will eat up time and could fail to make all your points.

Avoid moving about too much. Although some movement helps to keep the audience engaged, pacing up and down can be distracting.

At the end of your presentation ask if there are any questions. Listen carefully. If a question is complicated, rephrase it to simplify it without changing the meaning. For example: "I think you're asking me two things. Firstly, are confidence and self esteem the same thing? Secondly, if they are separate things, can you have one without the other? Am I right, is that what you want to know?"

* * * * *

Make meetings matter with mindfulness

Have you been asked to chair a meeting? Too often, meetings are boring and unfocused; they get bogged down in detail or derailed by side issues that drain everyone's energy and deter decision making. These meetings are mindless!

Instead, they should be about encouraging people to be open to each others' views and experiences and to move forward with clear action points.

Annie was part of a residents group that had raised funds to buy the local community hall. Annie was keen that once the hall was refurbished, a playgroup was reinstated. Jo, who was chairing the meeting, asked if there were any different views.

Louise said that she felt a playgroup would dominate daytime use of the hall.

Also, in the last few years several nurseries had opened in the area. Perhaps something else would be appropriate – a parent and toddler group maybe? Initially Annie found it difficult to let go of the idea of a playgroup – in fact the main reason she'd got involved in the group was because she wanted other families to benefit in the same way hers had. However, she quickly recognized that her ideas and feelings were part of the past; it was better to let them go and move forward.

How can you make sure the next meeting is an opportunity to share ideas and opinions, ensure that objections get heard and responded to and that plans and decisions are made?

Here are some tips to help you take a mindful approach to meetings.

1. Send out the agenda.

Be sure that it clearly and succinctly sets out the aims of the meeting; the issues to be discussed and the decisions to be made. This helps to ensure that everyone knows what the point and focus of the meeting will be.

2. Avoid rushing to the meeting.

A few minutes before the meeting, centre yourself. Stop what you are doing and breathe. This provides an opportunity to create a mindful space and remove any distractions – emails to write, phone calls to return etc. – that may make it difficult to be fully present in the meeting. One technique that may help is to write down on paper the task or issue you were in the middle of and then put it to one side. This simple act has the effect of allowing the issue to be laid aside until you pick it up again when the meeting is over.

3. Open with a clear objective and keep it focused.

Begin the meeting by restating the intentions and objectives of the meeting. "The purpose of this meeting is to decide . . . and . . .".

For some meetings, it might be appropriate to suggest that "We make decisions based on what we know *now* with the understanding that if new information comes to light later, we can change and adapt accordingly."

Keep the focus of the meeting, avoiding any discussion of topics unrelated to the stated purpose. If the meeting starts to veer away, suggest a "parking space" – a visible space where other issues are written down for discussion at another time.

Don't let things drag on; know when to stop someone. If there's been a long discussion, a disagreement or things are getting heated, propose the action that could be taken next: "Would it help if . . .", "How about we . . .", or "Can we at least agree that . . .".

4. Listen carefully.

Use the mindful listening techniques from the last chapter. If you are unclear, paraphrase what you have heard and ask for clarification. Ask for examples to illustrate or back up points or ideas.

5. Be aware of people's body language and other forms of non-verbal communication. If someone is looking confused, ensure that they have an opportunity to clarify their understanding.

Encourage questions for clarification, but be aware of questions that simply take the focus of the discussion off the point.

Ask the quieter members what their responses, ideas and opinions are. If other people aren't being heard say "I'd like to hear what . . . thinks".

6. Wrap up the meeting with clear action points.

As the meeting comes to a close, ensure everybody is clear about what will happen next, what people have committed themselves to and what the intended outcome is. Manage a meeting mindfully and it's more likely that something worthwhile will be achieved.

In a nutshell

- Prepare for meetings, interviews and presentations. Rather than worry about it, identify what might happen that you can prepare for now.
- Listen to other people's questions, ideas and suggestions. Use mindful listening techniques. Don't let your

thoughts distract or influence how well you listen. If you are unclear, paraphrase what you have heard and ask for clarification.

- Just before an interview or presentation, use positive self-talk: "I can do this. It will be fine". Breathe. Use a breathing technique that works for you.
- Explain your thoughts and ideas clearly and calmly. Try not to mumble or rush.
- When things don't go well, don't spend the rest of the day going back over things you should or shouldn't have done. Instead, focus on what you've learnt from the situation that you can put to good use next time.

Conclusion

Two monks are sitting side by side, meditating. The younger one is giving the older one a quizzical look, to which the older one responds, "Nothing happens next. This is it."

It's true. Mindfulness isn't about getting somewhere. It is simply a matter of knowing where you already are; that you're already there.

Awareness – being conscious and alert to thoughts, experiences and events that are happening right now – is, of course, one of the key principles of mindfulness.

So too are acceptance and acknowledgement; being able to understand that things are (or are not) happening and that thoughts, feelings and actions, etc. are just that: thoughts, feelings and actions.

Along with awareness, acceptance and acknowledgement, you will have read in this book that other aspects of mindfulness, such as focus and engagement, patience and trust, all contribute to helping you to live in the moment.

Hopefully you will you will have discovered a range of ideas and suggestions to help you apply these mindfulness principles and techniques.

It's important to emphasize, however, that it doesn't matter where you start and which aspect of mindfulness you use. What *is* important is simply to remember to start putting one of those aspects into practice!

Try out different strategies at different times and in different situations. Take a "beginner's mind" approach; open yourself to new ways of thinking and doing. Be prepared for new possibilities in familiar situations.

Remember, noticing and doing things in a new way puts you in the here and now because you are more aware of what's happening right now.

Be patient with yourself as you learn how to be more mindful; it takes time, genuine intention and commitment. But also don't forget that mindfulness is the ultimate mobile device – you can take it with you anywhere and use it at any time.

Just know that each time you are mindful in one situation, in the short term you'll manage that immediate situation calmly and clearly – and you'll feel more grounded and centred. Then, in the long term, each time you are mindful, you will be developing a way of thinking and doing that will become normal for you; your usual way of thinking and behaving.

With time you'll automatically bring mindfulness to your thoughts, words and actions and ultimately everything you do, so that whatever you think and do, mindfulness becomes how you live your life.

And remember, life unfolds in the present. There is never a time when your life is not now, in this moment. The present moment is life itself!

References

1. The Health & Social Care Information Centre, 2009, *Adult Psychiatric Morbidity in England: Results of a Household Survey*, Table 2.4, p. 41
2. Killingsworth, M. and Gilbert, D. T. 2010, "A wandering mind is an unhappy mind", *Science*, Vol. 330 no. 6006, p. 932
3. Cromie, W. J. 2006, "Meditation found to increase brain size", *Harvard Science*, February 2006, Vol. 2 http://news.harvard.edu/gazette/story/ 2006/02/meditation-found-to-increase-brain-size/
4. DiClemenet, C.C. and Prochaska, J.O. 1982, "Self change and therapy change of smoking behavior: A comparison of processes of change in cessation and maintenance", *Addictive Behaviors*, Vol. 7 no. 2, p. 133–42
5. Wohl, M., Pychyl T.A. and Bennett, S.H. 2010 "I forgive myself, now I can study: How self-forgiveness for procrastinating can reduce future procrastination." *Personality and Individual Differences*, Vol. 48, p. 803–808.
6. Shiv, B. and Fedorikhin, A. 1999, "Heart and mind in conflict: The interplay of affect and cognition in consumer decision making", *Journal of Consumer Research*, Vol. 26: December 1999
7. Muraven, M., et al. 1999 "Longitudinal improvement of self-regulation through practice: Building self-control strength through repeated exercise", *Journal of Social Psychology*, Vol. 139 no. 4, p. 446–57
8. Bowen S. and Marlatt A. 2009 "Surfing the urge: brief mindfulness-based intervention for college student smokers", *Psychology of Addictive Behaviour*, Vol. 23 no. 4, p. 666–71.
9. Boston, W. 2010 "Q&A Yoko Ono", Time Entertainment, 10 September 2010, http://www.time.com/time/arts/article/0,8599,2017363,00 .html#ixzz2Dd1lR5co
10. Santos, M. D., Leve, C. and Pratkanis, A. R., 1994, "Hey Buddy, can you spare seventeen cents? Mindful persuasion and the pique technique", *Journal of Applied Social Psychology*, Vol. 24 no. 9, p. 755–847

About the Author

Gill Hasson is a teacher, trainer and writer. She has 20 years experience in the area of personal development. Her expertise is in the areas of confidence and self-esteem, communication skills, assertiveness and resilience.

Gill delivers teaching and training for education organizations, voluntary and business organizations and the public sector.

Her writing includes books on the subject of resilience, communication skills, assertiveness and emotional intelligence.

Gill's particular interest and motivation is in helping people to realize their potential; to live their best life!

Acknowledgements

Thanks to Iain Campbell and Jonathan Shipley for the opportunity to write this book.

Thanks to my editor Jenny Ng for being able to differentiate the wood from the trees and pulling it altogether.

Index

acceptance   9, 14–15, 29, 30–1, 44,
    67–74, 82–3, 93, 96–7, 107–10,
    112–13, 117–19, 122–3, 130–2,
    146, 173–7, 180, 184–96
acknowledgement   9, 29, 67–71,
    80–1, 104–10, 112–13, 117–19,
    122–3, 148–9, 157, 168, 176–7,
    179–80, 195–6
actions   29, 30–1, 36–8, 46–8,
    55–6, 63–7, 74, 77–93, 111, 115,
    120–1, 144–57, 171, 175, 192,
    195–6
adrenaline   63, 117
agreeing to disagree   168–9, 180
alone, loneliness   133–9
alternate-nostril breathing
    technique   79
amygdala   104
anchoring oneself in the present
    moment   68, 74, 89–90
anger   27, 47, 62–3, 64, 68, 69,
    99–110, 123, 172–7
anxiety   3, 5–6, 9, 14, 23–5, 27, 38,
    62–3, 66–7, 88, 90, 96–7, 99–102,
    110–19, 121–3, 127–8, 183–93
apologies   110, 175
art   51–2, 65–7, 87–90, 134–6
assertiveness   106–7, 123, 199
automatic behaviours   13, 15, 36–7,
    39, 46–8, 54, 85, 153
awareness   4–8, 13, 21–2, 26, 29,
    30–1, 44, 45, 48, 50, 62–71, 74,
    81, 82–5, 88–90, 93, 96–7,
    103–10, 130–2, 137–9, 156–7,
    173–80, 183–93, 195–6

beginner's mind   7, 30–1, 35, 49–54,
    57, 72–3, 74, 89–90, 92–3, 96–7,
    113–14, 123, 131–2, 139, 154,
    196
behaviours   13, 15, 36–7, 39, 46–8,
    54, 63–7, 77–93, 96
bird-song   27–8, 90
blame mind trap   38, 43–4, 62–3, 68,
    122–3, 166
the body   63–7, 72–3
books   65–7, 90, 115–16, 119
boredom   15, 25, 28, 88, 134
brain structure   46–8, 53–4, 92, 104,
    149–52
the breath   4, 22, 74, 77–81, 103–12,
    116–19, 123, 154–7, 177, 185–6,
    188, 191, 193

calmness   25, 27, 52–4, 63, 96,
    102–10, 115, 132–4, 166–70,
    183–5, 193, 196
catastrophizing mind trap   38, 130,
    153, 187–8, 193
change stages   54–7, 185, 187–8
changing the way one thinks   7, 30–1,
    35, 41–3, 46–57, 72–3, 74, 89–90,
    92–3, 96–7, 113–14, 121–3,
    130–2, 139, 148–9, 154, 196
chattering minds   5, 15, 23, 25
children   21, 44–5, 48–9, 85, 115–16,
    120–3, 136, 145
chocolate-meditation exercise   82
clarification of criticisms   167, 180
clarity   4, 167, 180, 186, 192, 193,
    196

cluttered minds   26
colour-breathing technique   79
comfort zones   49
commenting minds   5, 15, 23, 25
communications   161–80, 181–93,
   199
computers   6, 23–4, 37, 44, 56, 80,
   83, 119, 151, 162
confidence   15, 28, 96–7, 127–32,
   161–2, 183–93, 199
confirmation mind trap   38, 40–1,
   49
conformity mind trap   38, 41–2, 49
contentment   90–2, 134–9
control issues   38, 104, 115, 132, 166,
   174
counter attacks, criticisms   168,
   179–80
creativity   50–4, 65–7, 90, 106, 134–5
criticisms   96–7, 159–62, 166–72,
   179–80
cycling activities   49, 57, 105, 116–19,
   133–5, 137

dancing, flow activities   89
daylight   27–8, 52, 62, 137, 151
debts   129
decision-making   6, 26, 39, 41, 46–7,
   107–10, 148–9, 172, 183–4,
   191–3
denial   14, 71
depression   5–6, 9, 14, 67
detached feelings   15
distractions   73, 80–1, 83, 116, 162,
   166, 178, 189, 191, 193
doing   7–8, 22–3, 29, 30–1, 35, 41–3,
   46–57, 72–93, 96–7, 113–14, 123,
   131–2, 139, 148–9, 151–4, 196
doubts   9, 15, 28, 112–13
driving activities   4, 15, 27–8, 37, 38,
   39–40, 44–5, 48–52, 68, 84–5
duration of meditations   61–2, 84
dying   3

eating   4, 37, 45, 48–9, 56, 80, 82–6,
   88–9, 146, 177
emails   44, 56, 83, 147, 150–1, 168,
   191
emotions   3–9, 13, 14–15, 24–30, 47,
   62–73, 81, 93, 99–123, 133–9,
   164, 166–77, 199
empathy   28–9, 46, 74, 109–10,
   162–6, 183–4
the emperor's new clothes   41–2
emptying one's head by writing down
   worries   114–15, 123, 168
engagement   9, 21, 28–9, 30, 87–90,
   93, 96–7, 104–10, 116, 134–9,
   185–93, 195–6
enjoyment   8, 27, 91–2, 101, 131–2,
   135–9, 145–6, 153, 183–6
everyday activities   4, 8, 13–15, 27–8,
   37, 44–5, 48–9, 82–7, 135, 151–4
experiences   3, 4–5, 6, 8, 23–8, 29,
   39–40, 49–54, 65–71, 74, 80–1,
   87–90, 97, 113–19, 128–9, 134–9,
   145–6, 176–7, 190, 195–6

fears   62–3, 65–7, 71, 81, 102,
   108–10, 114–19, 123, 127–8, 132,
   138–9, 149
feedback   88–90, 132, 186, 187–93
feelings   4, 7, 8–9, 13, 14–15, 24,
   25–7, 28–30, 47, 48, 57, 59–74,
   77–81, 92–3, 96, 99–123, 133–9,
   165–72, 173–7, 183–93, 195–6
films, flow activities   90
fishing, flow activities   90
flexible thinking   26, 46–57, 86,
   113–14, 148–9, 152–4, 157,
   183–93, 196
flow activities   87–90, 116, 132,
   134–9
focus   9, 15, 22, 25–30, 39–40, 44,
   47, 61–2, 65–7, 73, 78–9, 80–3,
   87–90, 92–3, 96–7, 102, 106–11,
   116–19, 123, 131–9, 143–57,

Index

163–6, 171, 178–80, 183–4, 187–96

football, flow activities 89, 135

forgiveness 15, 97, 121–3, 159–62, 173–7, 180

frustration 70, 103–10, 162, 173–7

the future 3, 4–6, 13–14, 22–5, 37–40, 44–5, 62, 66–71, 78, 80, 87, 90–2, 101–2, 110–23, 127–39, 144, 183–93

games and puzzles, flow activities 90, 132

gardening activities 44, 83, 84–5, 90, 134–5, 137

giving criticism 169–72, 180

giving to others 49, 92, 135–9, 177–80

goals 14–15, 28, 40, 46, 55–6, 87–90, 97, 115, 132, 134–9, 141–9, 151, 157, 177–80, 191–3

good things in life 8, 27, 91–2, 131–2, 153

gratitude 90–2, 127–8

guilt feelings 14–15, 26–7, 47, 62–7, 71, 96, 99–102, 119–23, 127, 129, 131

habits 25, 36–7, 46–9, 50–4, 56–7, 64, 85, 117–19, 153–7

happiness 24–5, 27, 40, 63–6, 91–2, 127–8, 131–2, 134–9, 153

Harrison, George 3

health issues 3, 112, 113, 114, 119–20, 144, 146, 147

helping others 49, 135–9

here and now 3–6, 8–9, 13–14, 21–3, 25, 27, 29–30, 35, 44–5, 52–4, 71, 74, 78–81, 119, 144, 165, 195–6

hobbies/sports/pastimes 15, 44–5, 89–90, 132, 134–9

hopelessness 127, 130–2, 138–9

housework activities 4, 8, 13, 14, 37, 44–5, 48–9, 56, 83–5, 88, 135, 151–4, 177

human/animal contrasts 22–3

impulsive reactions 104–10, 123, 154–7

Internet 44, 51, 56, 83, 136, 138, 147, 150–1, 168, 171, 191

interviews 44–5, 97, 119, 181–6, 192–3

intuition 71–3, 165–6

jealousy 14–15, 70, 172, 173–4

judgements 5, 13, 15, 22–3, 26–30, 39, 41, 45–6, 50, 67–8, 70–1, 74, 78, 80–1, 103–4, 109–10, 130–2, 153, 157, 164, 171–2

judo, flow activities 89

jumping-to-conclusions mind trap 38, 39, 62–3, 110, 130, 153

learning 3–4, 28, 31, 48, 57, 74, 87, 104–5, 113–14, 121–3, 130–9, 144, 167–8, 176–80, 184–93

letting go 7, 9, 27–30, 43, 46, 53, 57, 74–9, 80–1, 85, 93, 97, 102, 112, 119, 121–3, 162, 172–6, 180, 183–6, 190

listening 15, 28–9, 73–4, 106–7, 109–10, 159–69, 172, 179–80, 186–93

living in/for the moment contrasts 6, 21, 35, 52–3, 78–9, 87–8, 89–90, 195–6

loneliness 15, 127–8, 132–9

making space 86, 102, 105–10, 152–3, 155, 191–2

managing criticism 159–62, 166–72, 179–80

meditation   4, 23, 47, 61–2, 82–3,
   195
meetings at work   38–9, 44–5, 96,
   113, 136, 181–4, 189–93
memories   53–4, 66–7, 80, 173–7
meta-cognition   62–71, 112–13
the mind   23–5, 31, 36–7, 46–57,
   61–2, 72–3, 149–50
mind traps   37–46, 48, 62–7, 70–1,
   130–2, 145–6, 148–9, 153, 157,
   187–8, 193
mindfulness
   see also acceptance;
      acknowledgement; awareness;
      beginner's mind; engagement;
      focus; here and now; letting go;
      patience; trust
   brain structure   46–8, 53–4, 92,
      104, 149–52
   definition   3–5, 6, 7, 8, 21, 25–8,
      29–31, 153, 195–6
mindlessness   7, 37, 50–1, 53–4, 56,
   88, 177–80, 189–90
misunderstandings   74, 109–10,
   133–4, 165
mobile devices   6, 23–4, 37, 51, 56,
   68, 106, 119, 162, 191, 196
monks-meditating story   195
motivations   14–15, 28, 46, 97, 101,
   127–8, 137, 141–57, 159–62,
   177–80, 199
moving on   92–3, 122–3, 131–2, 172,
   176–7, 180, 190–3
music   49, 50, 53, 65–6, 89, 105–6,
   119, 135–6

negativity   26, 38, 65–6, 111–19, 123,
   127–39, 146, 153–4, 157, 168,
   179, 183–4
neurons   36–7, 46–8, 53–4, 92, 104
new ways of thinking and doing   7,
   30–1, 35, 41–3, 46–57, 72–4,

   89–93, 96–7, 113–14, 123, 131–2,
   139, 154, 196
non-doing   22–3, 29, 80–1, 84
non-judgement   5, 13, 15, 22, 23,
   26–30, 45, 67–8, 70–1, 74, 78,
   80–1, 103–4, 109–10, 130–2, 153,
   157, 164, 171–2
non-verbal communications (NVCs)
   163, 165–6, 189, 192

observations   80–1, 112–13, 119
Ono, Yoko   175
other-people interactions   4–5, 9, 15,
   26–9, 40–53, 56, 65, 74, 85, 96–7,
   106–10, 113–16, 128–9, 132–9,
   144–5, 159–80, 183–93

paintings   51, 90, 134–5
park-bench exercise   80–1, 112–13,
   119
the past   3–6, 13–14, 22–8, 30–1,
   37–8, 40, 43–7, 51–2, 62, 66–71,
   78, 80, 87, 90–2, 101–23, 127–8,
   130–9, 144, 154, 173–7, 184–5,
   190–3
patience   15, 30, 57, 93, 96–7, 147–9,
   195–6
personal development   9, 199
perspectives   28, 30–1, 38,
   42–3, 46–57, 109–10, 113–14,
   129–39, 148–9, 154, 169–72,
   183–4
persuading others   159–62, 177–80
photographs   51–2
physical aspects of emotions   63–7,
   72–3, 81, 92–3, 103–6, 117–19
physical exercises   116–19, 134–5,
   144, 149, 151–3
pink-elephant exercise   111
plans   4–5, 13–14, 22–3, 55–6, 63,
   85–6, 115, 143–57, 185–93
plasticity of the brain   47–8, 53–4

positivity   8, 49, 64–7, 71, 91–3,
    101–2, 121, 127–32, 146–9,
    153–4, 157, 176–7, 179–80, 193
the practice of mindfulness   8–9, 53,
    57, 93, 95–196
prejudice   41, 50, 110, 164
the present   3–8, 13–14, 21–9, 38,
    44–5, 51–4, 61–2, 66–71, 74,
    78–81, 83, 85, 87–92, 102–23,
    144, 152–4, 165, 173–7, 183–96
presentations at work   96, 181–4,
    186–9, 192–3
pride   64–6, 127–8
prioritization   85–6, 152
problem-solving, worrying
    contrasts   115

raisin-meditation exercise   82
reading activities   21, 83, 134–5
reflective listening   106, 162–7, 172,
    179–80, 192–3
reframing situations, anger
    management   107–8
relapses, change efforts   56–7
relationships   4–5, 9, 15, 26–9, 40–53,
    56, 65, 74, 85, 96–7, 106, 113,
    115–16, 128–9, 132–9, 144–5,
    159–80, 183–93
religion   137–8, 139
resentment   14–15, 70, 107–10,
    120–3, 138–9, 169–72, 173–7
resisting things, willpower uses   154–7
respect   107, 171
responsibilities   6, 25, 104–10, 122–3
responsive/reactive contrasts   26–7,
    30, 106–8, 110, 123, 167–8, 172,
    177–8, 186
rock climbing, flow activities   89, 135
routines   4, 14–15, 28, 46–9, 50–4,
    56, 85–7, 177
rumination   5–7, 14, 23, 111–19,
    121–3, 130–2, 133–9, 168

running   88–9, 105–6, 117, 143,
    146–7

sadness   65–7, 128, 132–9
self-acceptance   130–2
self-actualization   65–7
self-consciousness   88, 132, 186–9
self-doubt   9, 15, 28, 112–13,
    129–32
self-esteem   15, 28, 125–39, 183–4,
    189, 199
self-forgiveness   121–3
self-talk   26, 128–32, 139, 153–4,
    157, 188–9, 193
the senses   4, 22, 27–8, 47, 49–54,
    65–7, 71–3, 82–5, 89–90, 165–6
serotonin   63
sex   24
shaking-hands breathing technique
    79
shame   65, 70, 131
silence   4, 61, 80, 165
simple activities, willpower
    requirements   151–4, 157
singing   89, 105–6, 135, 137–8
single/multi-task activities   85–6, 152,
    157
sitting-up straight   151
skills   88–90, 128–39, 179–80
sleep   111
The Slow Movement   86
slowing down   85–7, 103–4, 105–10,
    152–4, 157, 179, 186, 189, 191,
    193
small pleasures in life   8, 27, 91–2,
    101, 131–2, 153
smiling   185
smoking   149, 155–7
spirituality   137–9
starting one's own business   63, 143
sticky notes   49, 80
stillness   4, 80

stress 3–9, 14–15, 25, 67, 72, 85, 88, 90, 97, 107, 111–23, 178, 183–4, 186–93
successes 56, 69, 88, 97, 134, 143, 147, 152, 154, 157
sunk-costs mind trap 38, 42–3, 148
support groups 138–9
"surfing the urge" resistance technique 155–6, 157
swimming, flow activities 89, 134–5, 154

talking over one's worries 106, 115–16
tax returns 149–50
tea-making activities 13, 84–5
teeth-brushing activities 8, 37, 84–5, 91
tennis, flow activities 89, 135
thinking diaries 44–5
"thinking outside the box" approaches 52–4
"This, too, shall pass!" approach to worry 115–16
thoughts 4, 7–9, 13–14, 22–5, 29–31, 35–7, 40–1, 44–57, 59–74, 77–81, 89–90, 92–3, 96, 101–2, 111–23, 156, 166, 183–93, 195–6
three-gates Arab proverb on giving criticism 170–1
trust 30, 57, 65, 93, 96–7, 127–8, 147–9, 175, 195–6
tunnel-thinking mind trap 38, 39–40, 62–3, 130, 145, 153

uncertainties 112–13, 186–93
uneasy mental images 72–3
unusual requests, persuading others 177–80
urges, "surfing the urge" resistance technique 155–6, 157

volunteering 49, 136–9, 177–80

waiting-time activities 52–3
walking activities 4, 14–15, 37, 48–9, 84–5, 105–6, 117–19, 135, 137, 151–4
wandering minds 61–2, 80–1, 84–5, 87–8, 116, 117, 119, 134–5
washing-up activities 8, 14–15, 83–5, 151–2, 169
willpower 14–15, 46, 141–4, 149–57
work 3–6, 9, 15, 38, 40–5, 52–4, 63, 91, 96, 111–12, 119, 128–9, 132, 143–4, 150–1, 177–80, 181–93
worry 5–6, 9, 22–5, 27, 38, 46–7, 54–5, 62–3, 66–9, 80, 96–7, 99–102, 110–19, 123, 127–9, 183–93
worry time 102, 116, 123
worst-case scenarios 14, 38, 113, 115
writing 114–15, 123, 134–5, 143, 147, 168, 191

yoga, flow activities 89, 116, 134–5

Zen proverbs 85